Your **North Node number(s)**

To find your **North Node number(s)** you overlay your astrological natal/birth chart on the circle grid on page 264 of the book Numerology and the Divine Triangle by Faith Javane and Dusty Bunker, and see which number(s) your North Node lands on (of the 36 possible places one's North Node can land on: 12 have two numbers (which work synergistically), and the other 24 have one number).

Again, let's use the following birth data as an example:

Michael Eugene Byrne

born on November 30th, 1954

at 12:14 a.m. in Newark, Ohio

For obtaining natal charts, I prefer to use:

www.astro.com

On the upper left hand side, click on: Astrology Atlas Query

And on the submenu, click on: Time Zone Atlas, Horoscope of the Moment

Type in the city (location) of birth

Click on the correct state (location) of birth

Enter the birth data and click: continue

Click on: Extended Chart Selection

Tick the box: always use True Node

Click on: Click here to show the chart

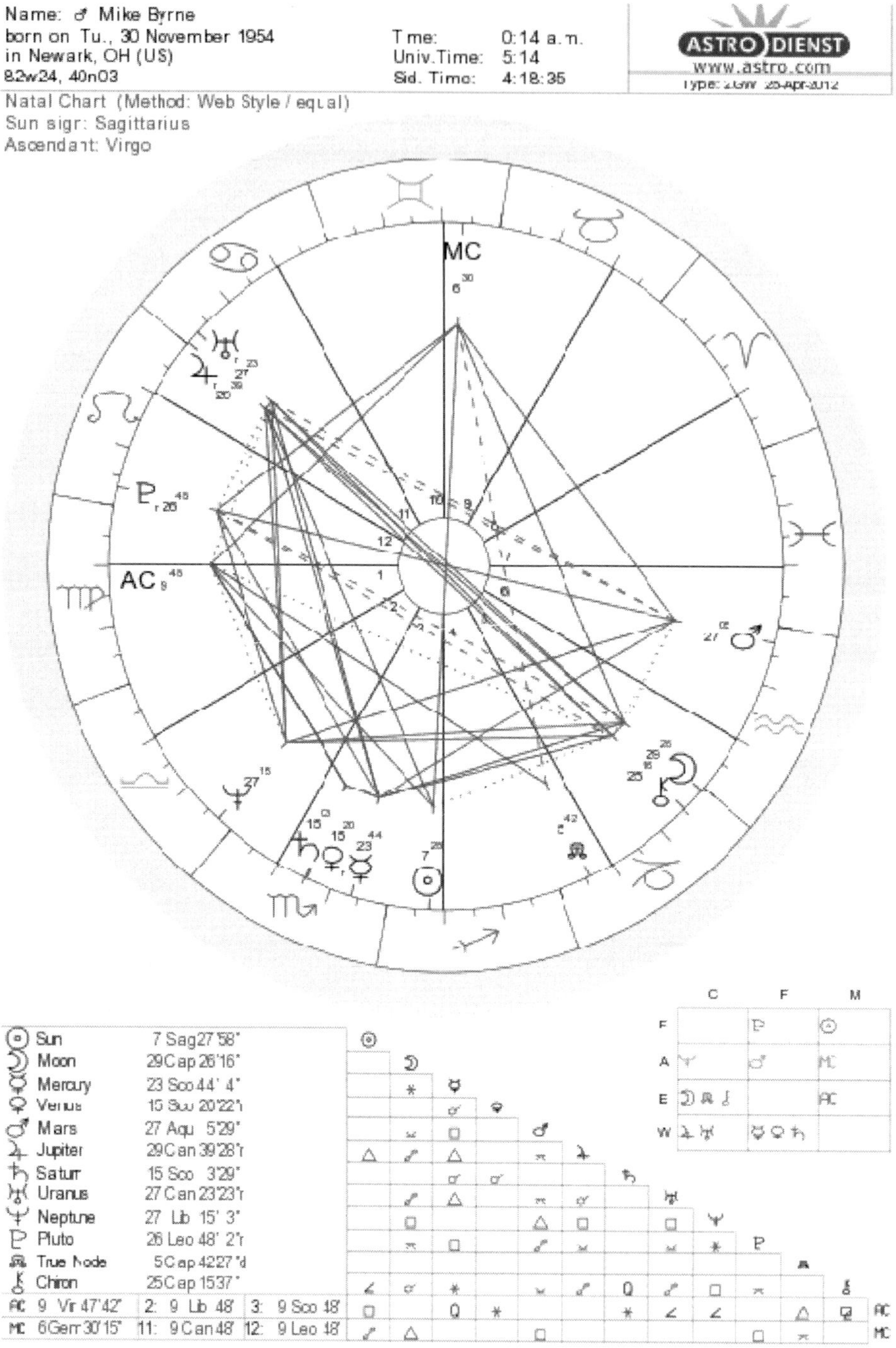

On this site, the North Node looks somewhat like a light blue horseshoe.

Mike's North Node at 5 degrees in Capricorn is in the third decan (last 10 degrees) of the fourth house. So his North Node numbers are **40** and **44**.

Your **South Node number(s)** and **North Node number(s)**

Astrologically one's South Node tells you what has always worked for you in the past and what your normal approach to life is. Whereas astrologically one's North Node points the way toward your continuing growth and development as a person. Engaging the approach to life indicated by one's North Node is challenging but rewarding.

Similarly, one's South Node number tells you numerologically what approach to life has always worked for you in the past, while numerologically one's North Node number indicates what approach to life will further your continuing growth and development as a human being.

Astrologically one's South and North Nodes are 180 degrees (or exactly 6 signs) apart. Similarly, numerologically one's South and North node numbers differ by 28 (two suits of the tarot).

Numerologically the Node numbers range from 23 to 78. So if your North Node number is between 23 and 50, then you add 28 to your North Node number to find your South Node number. If your North Node number is between 51 and 78, then you subtract 28 to find your South Node number.

For example:

Michael Eugene Byrne born November 30th, 1954 at 12:14 a.m. in Newark, Ohio.

Name: ♂ Mike Byrne
born on Tu., 30 November 1954
in Newark, OH (US)
82w24, 40n03

Time: 0:14 a.m.
Univ.Time: 5:14
Sid. Time: 4:18:35

ASTRO DIENST
www.astro.com
Type: 2.GW 25-Apr-2012

Natal Chart (Method: Web Style / equal)
Sun sign: Sagittarius
Ascendant: Virgo

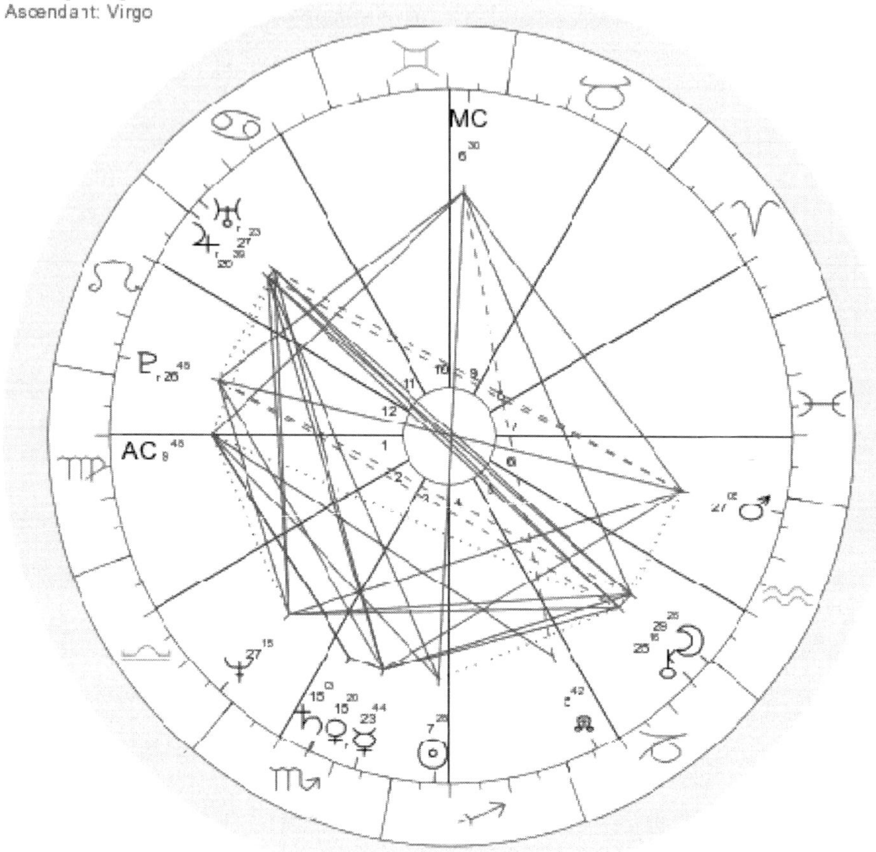

Sun	7 Sag 27'58"				
Moon	29 Cap 26'16"				
Mercury	23 Sco 44' 4"				
Venus	15 Sco 20'22"r				
Mars	27 Aqu 5'29"				
Jupiter	29 Can 39'28"r				
Saturn	15 Sco 3'29"				
Uranus	27 Can 23'23"r				
Neptune	27 Lib 15' 3"				
Pluto	26 Leo 48' 2"r				
True Node	5 Cap 42'27"d				
Chiron	25 Cap 15'37"				
AC	9 Vir 47'42"	2:	9 Lib 48'	3:	9 Sco 48'
MC	6 Gem 30'15"	11:	9 Can 48'	12:	9 Leo 48'

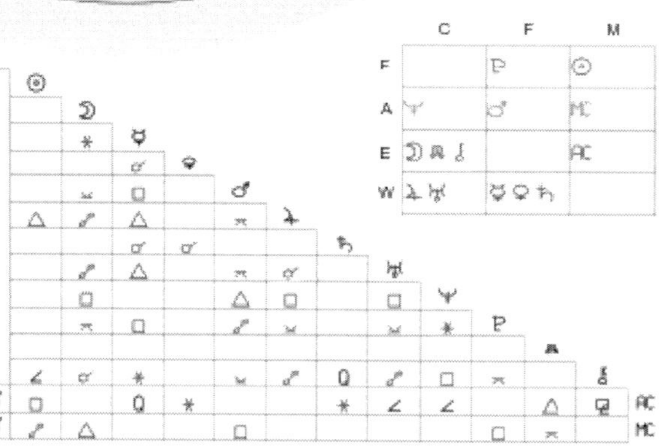

His North Node is at 5 degrees in the sign of Capricorn in the third decan (last ten degrees) of the 4th house, and his South Node is at 5 degrees in the sign of Cancer in the third decan (last ten degrees) of the 10th house.

Using the chart on page 264 of the book Numerology and the Divine Triangle by Faith Javane and Dusty Bunker reveals this his **South Node numbers** are **68** and **72** (third decan of the 10th house), while his **North Node numbers** are **40** and **44** (third decan of the 4th house). His normal 68/72 approach to life (perhaps as a lifelong student (68) who is thrifty (72)) has already been learned, and though it is challenging (but rewarding) – for his personal growth and development his North Node numbers (40/44) call him to be helpful and of service (40) and to be self-aware, to meditate and to have his finger on the pulse of what's happening (44).

This is a list of descriptions of the numbers **23 to 78**. Following the numbers 23 through 78 in parentheses is the tarot card that corresponds to that number.

23 (King of Wands) Leadership. Zest. Action. Exercise. Physical fitness. Working out. Gym. Calisthenics. Physicality. Athletic. Athlete. Sports. Entrepreneur. Self-starter. Enterprising. Small businessperson. Yelling. Temper tantrums.

24 (Queen of Wands) Dominance. Clean living. Wholesome. Fit & trim. Devotion. Vows. Pledge. Commitment. Purity. Nutrition. Nourishment. Clean diet. Whole foods. Organic foods. Natural living. Natural diet. Bodily purity. Nutrients. Vitamins. Supplements. Fortified. Self-contained. Abstinence. Celibacy. Chastity. Virgin. Pure. Demure. Modesty. Short hair. Clean cut. Crew cut. Drill instructor. Sergeant. Hammer. Claw. Catcher. Goalie. Goalkeeper. Dentist. Teeth. Floss. Toothpaste. Fluoride. FDA. Unadulterated. Sanitize. Disinfectant. Antiseptic. Housekeeping. Prune. Trim. Rooster. Henhouse. Hen. Mother hen. Henpeck. Queen bee. Puritanical. Prudish. Blush. Bashful. Submissive. Submission. Bow. Kneel. Collectivism. Communism.

25 (Knight of Wands) Adventure. Excitement. Thrilling. Exploring. Discover. Encourage. Activist. Advocate. A cause. Rooting. Encouragement. Free spirited. Perky. Movement. Relocate. Thrill seeker. Restless. Antsy.

26 (Page of Wands) Communication. Enthusiasm. Charisma. Personality. Popularity. Celebrity. Actress. Actor. Movies. Appearance. Image. Good-looking. Pretty. Handsome. Gorgeous. Attractive. Beauty. Model. Glamour. Glowing. Leonine. Comeliness. Camera. Photos. Photogenic. Photography. Headshot. Oral. Speech. Speak. Talk. Verbalize. Articulate. Orator. Public speaking. Conversation. Message. Information. News. Reports. Headlines. Broadcasting. Show. Television. The media. The press. Newspaper. Reporter. Antenna. Radio. Talk radio. Telephone. Phone call. Fax. Mail. A letter. A post. E-mail. Telegraph. Transmit. Send. Announcements. Posters. Placard. Publicity. Publicist. Spokesperson. Emcee. Cheerleader. Pep rally. Beauticians. Hair stylists. Haircut. Cosmetics. Adoring fans. Autograph. Signature. Personalize. Audience. Applaud. Applause. Cheer. Teleprompter. Pregnant. Head. Headshot. Header. Drama. Hollywood. Vanity. Narcissist. Ego. Publicity stunt.

27 (Ace of Wands) Initiative. Follow through. Original. The first. Innovation. Trailblazer. Pioneer. Inventor. Founder. Start. Begin. Usher in. Initiate. Debut. Groundbreaking. Drilling. Drill. Launch. Premiere. New start. Fresh start. First step. The beginning. Opening scene. Opening line. Kickoff. First pitch. Reset. Restart. Contraption.

28 (Two of Wands) Bold. Daring. Heroic. Survivor. Possibilities. Overcoming obstacles. Personal power. Willpower. Powerful. Superpowers. Unstoppable. Invincible. Bulletproof. Fearlessness . Daredevil. Weightlifting. Bodybuilder. Muscles. Audacity. Temerity. Vulnerability. Reckless. Same-sex. Lightweight. Pathetic. Weak. Feeble. Scrawny. Wimp.

29 (Three of Wands) Self-confidence. Self-assurance. Coordination. Adept. Skills. Talents. Competence. Expertise. Specialty. Proficient.

Capable. Combine. Synergy. Teamwork. Cooperation. Duo. Duet. Collaborate. Collaboration. Consult. Consultant. Participation. Participant. Architect. Blueprint. Master plan. Inept.

30 (Four of Wands) Thankfulness. Appreciation. Gratefulness. Gratitude. Cherish. Blessings. Please. Tha nk you. Alleluia! Lavish. Luxury. Castle. Palace. Abode. Home. Interior decorating. Decor. Adornments. Elegance. Spiffy. Style. Fashion. Clothing. Clothes. Attire. A pparel. Wardrobe. Outfits. Designer. Khaki. Shoes. Footwear. Soccer. Golf. Polo. Cricket. Ba dminton. Softball. Garden. Gardening. Grapes. Vineyard. Wine. Gourmet. Silver spoon. Ingrate.

31 (Five of Wands) Competition. Challenges. Tests. Contests. Contestant. Runner-up. Competitor. Contender. Opponent. Scrimmage. Sparring. Practice. Training. Cross-training. Trainer. Martial arts. Karate. Wrestling. Grappling. Arm bar. Drums. Scramble. Stir. Catalyst. Reaction. Chemistry. Reagents. Emulate. Striving. Risk . Controversy. Contention. Provocateur. Provoke. Instigate. Incite. Tease. Taunt. Noise. Diss onance. Cacophony. Commotion. Uproar. Ruckus. Dispute. Disturbance. Struggles. Strife. Sq uabbles. Scuffle. Quarrels. Altercation. Brawl. Donnybrook. Feuds. Antagonism. Antagonist. Rivalry. Agitation. Rowdy. Wild. Troublemaker. Rabble-rouser. Havoc. Skirmish. Riot. Scandal.

32 (Six of Wands) Winning. Victory. Triumph. Champion. Mighty. Glory. Pride. Top 10. First place. Number 1. Better. Exceptional. The greatest. The best. The biggest. Giant. Huge. Jumbo. Gigantic. Humongous. Colossal. Mammoth. Ginormous. Super -

sized. Goliath. Juggernaut. Behemoth. Monolithic. Blockbuster. Majority. Mainstream. Conformity. Consensus. Democracy. Freedom. Liberty. Independence. Autonomy. Sovereign. Self-determination. Declaration. March. Parade. Nationalism. Patriotism. Flags. Banners. Anthem. Olympics. Medal. Trophy. Awards. Crown. King. Apples. Baseball. Batter. Batting. Hitter. Hits. Home run. Grand slam. Slam dunk. MVP. Bingo. Basic. Simple. Easy. Ease. Convenience. Cushion. Gadgets. Gizmo. Shopping. Consumerism. Consumption. Capitalism. Bruiser. Boxing. Pugilism. Knuckles. Fists. Punch. Hit. Swing. Belt. Clobber. Wallop. Knockout. Fight. Battle. Combat. Pile on. Beat. Smackdown. Stomp. Kick. Impulsive. Self-indulgence. Glutton. Overeater. Bloated. Oversized. Gimme. Excuses. Belligerent. Bully. Arrogant. Reactionary. Shortsighted. Myopic. Anti-intellectualism. Sensationalism. Xenophobic. Orthodox. Imperialism. Colonialism. Tyranny.

33 (Seven of Wands) Courage. Bravery. Valor. Valiant. Magnanimous. Bighearted. Lionhearted. Backbone. Spine. Loyalty. Captain. Cowboy. Cowgirl. Cowboy hat. Hat trick. Big hat. Sombrero. Country. Ranch. Rodeo. Bulls. Wrangler. Bolero. Taco. Lion. Fierce. Roar. Moxie. Bravado. Machismo. Cojones. Bluster. Braggart. Buckle. Surrendering. Coward. Chicken. Gutless.

34 (Eight of Wands) Speed. Velocity. Rate. Pace. Quickness. Rapidity. Swiftness. Fastness. Dexterity. Agility. Footing. Nimble. Mobility. Texting. Cell phones. Frequency. Often. Energetic. Acceleration. Momentum. Locomotion. Quick. Quickly.

Exhilaration. Adrenaline. Wiry. Energy. Fuel. Kerosene. Gasoline. Motor. Engines. Rev. RPM. Combustion. Wiring. Circuit. Ignition. Battery. Transportation. Vehicle. Automobile. Cars. Motorist. Driving. Maneuver. Steering wheel. Motocross. BMX. Bicycle. Cyclist. Spinning. Ride. Saddle. Pedal. Brakes. Tires. Wheels. Traction. Motorcycle. Go-kart. Racing. Derby. Relay. Laps. Sprinting. Walk. Jog. Run. Stride. Pedestrian. Footing. Pavement. Asphalt. Road. Lane. Traffic. Commuters. Express. Trains. Locomotive. Subway. Railway. Bus. Shuttle. Airplane. Passenger. Flying. Pilot. Aviation. Flight. Parachute. Runway. Tarmac. Express. Urgent. Hurry. Rush. Busy. Zip. Zoom. Turbo. Boost. Dash. Dart. Tempo. Windmill. Hydraulic. Turbine. Pump. Funnel. Flow. Circulate. HVAC. Vent. Duct. Tube. Pipeline. Conduit. Cool. Heat. Boiler. Radiator. Antifreeze. Coolant. Thermostat. Therm. Fahrenheit. Celcius. Kelvin. Temperature. Thermometer. Warm. Toasty. Hot. Perspire. Sweat. Swelter. Simmer. Boil. Roast. Barbecue. Bake. Oven. Stove. Furnace. Crackling. Fiery. Singe. Scorch. Burn. Matches. Lighter. Kindle. Flame. Torch. Candle. Wick. Lit. Cloud. Smoke. Smoldering. Blaze. Fire. Firefighter. Fire

extinguisher. Flammable. Volatile. Combustible. Incendiary. Implosion. Tamp. Explosive. Bo om. Blast. Bullet. Gunpowder. Nitroglycerin. Dynamite. A
fuse. Pyrotechnics. Fireworks. Firecracker. Skyrocket. Meteoric. Free
fall. Revolve. Orbit. Satellite. Trajectory. Fleeting. Barrage. Volley. Canon. Consecutive. Stre ak. Rapid
fire. Incoming. Archery. Quiver. Arrow. Rocket. Missile. Silo. Torpedo. Launch. Fling. Catap ult. Slingshot. Propulsion. Thrust. Pitcher. Fastball. Paramotor. Paragliding. Airspace. Jet. H elicopter. Tilt. Torque. Propeller. Spin. Turn. Rotate. Whirl. Swirl. Twist. Twister. Tornado. Whirlwind. Unleash. Target. Bull's-
eye. Marksman. Aim. Point. Hop. Rabbit. Hare. Swerve. Metabolism. Mitochondria. Carboh ydrates. Calories. Royal
jelly. Honey. Hornets. Wasps. Buzzing. Humming. Hive. Swarm. Sting. Scratch. Itch. Rash. Skin. Flesh. Complexion. Dermatologist. Inflammation. Injection. Red. Redhead. Nozzle. Sip hon. Kidney. Adrenals. Cortisol. Stress. Tension. Nerves. High-
strung. Fry. Sizzle. Skillet. Boiling. Overheat. Melt. Blow
up. Erupt. Pop. Cap. Lid. Compressed. Pressure. Venting. Steam. Geyser. Gush. Leak. Spill.

Rupture. Volcano. Lava. Cone. Plume. Ash. Cinder. Spew. Flare. Fireball. Inferno. Wildfire. Heat wave. Hot
spell. Desert. Dry. Coal. Smokestack. Chimney. Aerosol. Propane. Methane. Fracking. Frictio n. Crash. Collision. Derail. Fizzle. Rajasic. Spicy. Chilies. Peppers. Capsaicin. Caliente. Onio ns. Garlic. Leeks. Chives. Alliums. Allicin. Sulfur. Stimulation. Stimulants. Smoking. Cigarett es. Tobacco. Nicotine. Percolate. Coffee. Caffeine. Wired. Hyper. Nitroglycerin. Fever. Lizard s. Temper. Hothead. Jealousy. Envy. Laxative.

35 (Nine of
Wands) Perseverance. Persistence. Endurance. Stamina. Resilience. Durability. Outlast. Cont inue. Duration. Distance. Farthest. Steady. Steadfast. Stay. Maintain. Consistency. Ongoing. Protein. Immune system. Antibodies. Immunity. Self-
defense. Defenses. Guarded. Shield. Safeguards. Vigilance. Preparations. Ready. Equip. Equi pment. Furnish. Provision. Tool
kit. Comeback. Activation. Efficacy. Effectiveness. Marathons. Local. Guarantee. Warranty. I nsurance. Inheritance. Trust fund. Heir(ess). Bequeath. Gatekeeper. Minor leagues. Junior varsity. Second
stringers. Rookies. Reinforce. Adhesive. Glue. Sustained. Resume. Continuity. Capacity. Rese rvoir. Insulation. Withstand. Dreadlocks. Deter. Alert. Warn. Warning. Threatening. Immine nt. Weary. Preemptive. Prevent. Intervention. Interrupt. Interception. Incomplete. Quarterba ck. Sacked. Concussion. Interim. Temporary. Short-
lived. Stopgap. Stop. Quit. Cessation. Give
up. Deplete. Draining. Grueling. Exhaustion. Fainting. Collapse. Passing

out. Dehydration. Headaches. Migraines. Overdo. Overexertion. Strain. Virulence. Virus. Flu. Antigen. Vaccine. Immunization. Innoculate. Antidote. Probiotics. Antibiotics. Infection. Inf ectious. Pathogen. Prevalence. Incidence.

36 (Ten of
Wands) Managing. Delegating. Workload. Elevation. Ascent. Hills. Cliffs. Massif. Ridge. Plat eau. Milestone. Capstone. Pinnacle. Apex. Precipice. Summit. Mountain. Mountaineering. Cli mbing. Climber. Hiking. Hiker. Trek. Encampment. Backpack. Luggage. Suitcase. Pack. Unp ack. Shoulders. Deltoids. Trapezius. Carry. Drag. Lug. Haul. Pull. Push. Shove. Tug. Press. Lift. Deadlift. Powerlifter. Strongest. Hulk. Bulk. Rocks. Stones. Pounds. Weight. Payload. Weight
load. Tonnage. Ton. Freight. Cargo. Container. Crates. Bins. Tubs. Stacking. Load. Pile. Inc rease. Decrease. Unearth. Earthmover. Bulldozer. Tank. Forklift. Pyramid. Cranes. Counterb alance. Fulcrum. Leverage. Raised. Arch. Bridge. Span. Pillars. Columns. Brace. Wedge. Fas ten. Swivel. Pivot. Pulleys. Rigger. Knot. Scaffolding. Enclosure. Overhead. Ceiling. Cover. T arp. Tent. Stake. Post. Pole. Bundle. Platform. Deck. Tether. Stretch. Extend. Bend. Handle. Grasp. Grip. Squats. Skull. Helmet. Skateboard. Roller
skate. Rollerblade. Wagon. Loading. Unloading. Crawl. Staircase. Stairs. Steps. Elevators. Es calators. Boulder. Stony. Rocky. Blocks. Slab. Marble. Granite. Chisel. Carve. Thickness. Inc remental. Doable. Reachable. Maximizing. Maximization. Maximum. Endeavor. Feats. Weigh ty responsibilities. Creditworthiness. Debt. Charge cards. Credit
cards. Mortgage. Obligations. Owe. Indebted. Credit limit. Credit rating. Credit score. FICO score. Credit rating
agency. Consolidation. Cutbacks. Deficit. Baggage. Burdens. Onerous. Cumbersome. Encumb ered. Sherpas. Yaks. Rhino. Yoke. Ox. Mule. Workhorse. Plow. Shovel. Dig. Wheelbarrow. T rench. Bunker. Wingspan. Brown. Spread. Fold. Unload. Drop. Dropkick. Adoption. Foster care. Orphan. Oppression. Difficulty. Mandatory. Verge. Edge. Brink. Precipice. Cliffhanger. Trample. Crunch. Compress. Compaction. Pulverize. Smash. Crushing. Backbreaking. Micro managing. Unmanageable. Overachiever. Surpass. Exceed. Beyond. Outreach. Overreaching. Overbearing. Overpower. Override. Megalomaniac. Dictator. Strongman. Heavy-
handed. Cudgel. Stick. Club. Gnarled. Gnarly. Siege. Recalls. Incumbent. Brinkmanship. Flip . Rollover. Topple. Crackdown. Corporal. Overdraft. Overdrawn. Default. Shutdown. Foreclo sure. Unbearable.

37 (King of Cups) Benevolence. Heartfelt. Heart-centered. Father. Dad. Fatherly
advice. Grandfather. Grandpa. Paternal. Parental. Paternity. Emotive. Music. Musician. Sing er. Singing. Songs. Tunes. Melodies. Voice. Guitar. Piscean. Osmosis. Hydration. Hydrophili c. Wet. Soak. Bathe. Bathtub. Shower. Faucet. Drip. Moisture. Wet. Splash. Swimming. Divi ng. Pools. Surfing. Surfboard. Waves. Aquatic. Fish. Fishing. Angler. Boat. Boating. Sailing. Ship. Ahoy. Sailor. Lake. River. Hydropower. Undulate. Waves. Buoy. Goggles. Bubbles. Fo

am. Tank. Aquarium. Watermelon. Hydroponic. Beverage. Water. Juicing. Liquidarian. . Guzzle. Imbibe. Drinking. Taverns. Pubs. Bars. Bartenders. Cocktails. Alcohol. Liquor. ze. Bottles. Drunkard. Lush. Liver. Bladder. Squirt. Pissy. Haters.

38 (Queen of Cups) Caring. Nurturing. Support. Feelings. Emotions. Mom. Mothering. Grandmother. Grandma. Maternal. Mother's intuition. Baby. Babying. Babysitting. Grab. Embrace. Hugs. Squeezing. Touching. Massage. Cuddling. Nuzzle. Nestle. Nest. Cocoon. Wrap. Blanket. Towel. Sensitive. Palpable. Taproot.

Trace. Echo. Mirror. Protect. Sheltering. Texture. Carton. Groceries. Deli. Cafeteria. Kitchen. Chef. Cook. Culinary. Cuisine. Cater. Cooking. Stomach. Digest. Burp. Sip. Lick. Suck. Feeding. Nurse. Milk. Lactation. Dairy. Cheese. Eggs. Lactose. Oxytocin. Hormones. Birthing. Coo(ing). Babbling. Arms. Hands. Mitt. Paw. Bear. Cubs. Nest. Cow. Udders. Mammal. Bosom. Cleavage. Chest. Clam. Crab. Claw. Octopus. Tentacles. Clamp. Suction. Cup. Jug. Bowl. Tray. Jiggle. Trunk. Rear end. Booty. Womb. Diaper. Absorb. Sponge. Soak. Swell. Heave. Squish. Wiggle. Squirm. Gel. Gooey. Sentimental. Attachment. Clinging. Affected. Pajamas. Hibernate. Ween. Coddle. Enabling. Codependency. Touchy. Pouting. Twisted. Perverse. Carcinogens. Oncology.

39 (Knight of Cups) Charm. Idealism. Ideals. Romantic. Dating. Dreamy. Bard. Poet. Poetic. Poetry. Lyrical. Lyrics. Rhymes. Compliments. Invitations. Offers. Proposals. Engagement. Fiancé. Fiancée. Dreamer. Utopia. Paradise. Idyllic. Dreamlike. Perfect. Nice. Commitments. Promises. Sincerity. Genuine. Authentic. Chivalry. Suitor. Woo. Courtship. Honeymoon. Serenade. Flirting. Bachelor(ette). Puppy. Cute. Fawning. Flattery. Storytelling. Storybook. Myths. Fables. Fairytales. Cinderella. Unicorns. Never-never land. Romanticize. Half-truths. Sycophant. Noncommittal. Bootlicker. Brownnoser.

40 (Page of Cups) Helpfulness. Assistance. Aid. Favor. Volunteering. Loving kindness. Goodwill. Gentle. Good Samaritan. Townspeople. Community. Neighborhood. Neighbors. Relatives. Kin. Siblings. Offspring. Son. Daughter. Grandchildren. Grandparents. Aunts. Uncles. Brotherhood. Service. Seva. Karma yoga. Service work. Civic duty. The common good. Altruism. Parks. Renovation. Remodeling. Jury duty. Helpers. Attendants. Servant. Doorman. Squire. Handmaiden. Maiden. Maid. Butler. Fetch. Bring. Waitstaff. Tips. Prince. Rescue. Princess. Doll. Fond. Tender. Scrumptious. Yummy. Dote. Pampered. Spoiled brat. Spoiled rotten. Puella. Welfare.

41 (Ace of Cups) Intimacy. Closeness. Familiarity. Availability. Arousal. Turn-on. Receiving love. First love. Fertility. Potency. Viability. Surrogate. Closure. Longing. Accept. Reject. One way love. Unrequited love. False heart. Cheating heart. Affair. Infidelity. Unfaithful. Adultery. Mistress. Threesome. Premature. Pre-marital sex. Exclude. Withdrawing. Withholding. Inadequacies. Turnoff. Unloved. Unwanted. Stigma. Frigidity. (Emotionally) unavailable. Cougar. Menopause. Sterility. Fertility issues. Pregnancy issues. Reproductive issues. Sexual dysfunctions. Contraception. Birth control. Ovulation. Fertilization. Conception. Embryo. Fetus. Prostate. Ovaries. Puberty. Menses. Cramp. Clot. Hemoglobin. Anemic. STDs.

42 (Two of Cups) Relationships. Love. Love life. Loving relationships. True love. Soul mates. Lovers. Couples. Consorts. Significant other. Spouse. Bride & groom. Wedding. Marriage. Matrimony. Marital. Deep sharing. Beautiful. Amorous. Lips. Kissing. Smooch. Intercourse. Making love. Having sex. Mating. Procreating. Copulation. Conjugal. Reproduction. Matching. Compatibility. Synastry. Mutuality. Reciprocal. Consensual. Permission. Likewise. Allies. Allegiance. Companion. Companionship. Together. Twosome. Bond(ing). Connect. Promiscuity. Misunderstandings.

43 (Three of Cups) Fun. Enjoyment. Playing. Celebrating. Entertainment. Entertaining. Fun times. Good times. Congratulations. Abundance. Bountiful. Enough. Plenty. Lots. Cornucopia. Sumptuous. Feast. Banquet. Cookouts. Picnic. Potluck. Banquet. Dinner. Host. A toast. Gregarious. Recreation. Hobby. Pastime. Leisure. Diversions. Festivities. Events. Fairs. Fairgrounds. Festival. Gala. Gatherings. Get togethers. Reunions. Satsang. Friendship. Friends. Peers. Colleagues. Cohort. Fellow. Chap. Mingle. Guests. Acquaintance. Pals. Buddies. Chummy. Hospitable. Hospitality. Birthday. Anniversary. Jubilee. Holidays. Merriment. Mirth. Frolicking. Amusement. Laughter. Chuckle.

Comedy. Funny. Cheerful. Festive. Partying. Jump. Choreography. Dancing. Ballet. Welcome. Greetings. Salutations. Hello. Hi. Hey. Handshake. Introduce. Introduction. Homophily. Belong. Join. Groups. Clubs. Performer. Trio. Bands. Crowds. Flock. Huddle. Meetings. Reunite. Liking. Gamer. Games. Toys. Playground. Playtime. Playful. Beach. Crowded. Overindulgence.

44 (Four of Cups) Meditating. Dhyana. Introspection. Self-awareness. Self-reflection. Looking inward. Noticing. Assessment. Relevant. Topical. Recent. Contemporary. Fresh. Happening. Update. Status. Condition. The moment. Real-time. Presently. Currently. Now. Today. Wide-open. In touch. In tune. Tone. Resonance. Acknowledge. Validate. Notify. Notifications. Feedback. Commentary. Comment. Diary. Journaling. Tumblr. Twitter. Tweeting. Blogging. Log. Self-

acceptance. Being oneself. Alright. Okay. Mellow. Chillin'. Sitting. Chair. Seat. Raja yoga. Padmasana. Trance. Zen. Acoustic guitar. Ukulele. Tuning. Ambient. Unplugged. Open. Reflexive. Savant. Re-evaluate. Self-absorbed. Self-conscious. Stale. Apathy. Ignore. Denial. Synesthesia.

45 (Five of Cups) Intensity. Focus. Concentration. Dharana. Depth. Deep. Profound. Toughness. Iron. Steel. Metal. Hardcore. True grit. Hardworking. Effort. Intentionality. Motivation. Psychology. Unflinching. Self-protective. Empowerment. Self-help. Self-improvement. Self-mastery. Do-it-yourselfer. Common sense. Streetwise. City. Recharge. Reenergize. Regeneration. Vegetarian. Repair. Mend. Fix. Premonitions. Mysteries. Secrets. Unexplained. Uncertainties. Enigma. Cryptic. Symbols. Subtle. Motive. Probe. Investigate. Detective. Mystic. Occult. Magic. Private. Privacy. Bedroom. Psychosexual. Penetrate. Magnetic. Attraction. Scorpionic. Powerful. Force. Magnitude. Amplify. Extreme. Ultra. Surge. Letting go. Cleanse. Purge. Catharsis. Apologies. I'm sorry. Hurt. Pain. Issues. Problems. Mistakes. Regret. Permanent. Indelible. Tattoos. Piercings. Needles. Scars. Blood. Filings. Shavings. Smudge. Mar. Stain. Trauma. Injury. Wound. Harm. Damage. Broken. Disappointment. Brooding. Seething. Resentment. Blame. Fault. Stare. Omen. Cringe. Wince. Heavy. Hardened. Hard knocks. Hook. Addiction. Painkillers. Habitual. Repeat. Chronic. Relapse. Compulsive. Hurtful. Self-destructive. Scary. Creepy. Workaholic. Controlling. Vindictive. Grudge. Revenge. Vendetta. Violence. Danger.

46 (Six of Cups) The past. Yesterday. Happy memories. Nostalgia. Child-like innocence. Age. Youth. Shorty. Kids. Maturity. Growing up. Adolescence. Adulthood. Cyclical. Seasons. Springtime. Bloom. Blossom. Roses. Flowers.

Bouquet. Corsage. Paisley. Arrival. Departure. Attendance. Schedule. Appointment. Promptness. Punctual. On time. Early. Waiting. Soon. Shortly. Later. When. Time. Hours. Minutes. Seconds. Timepiece. Clock. Wristwatch. Hourglass. Timer. Countdown. Calendar. Days. Weeks. Months. Years. Timeline. Timetable. History. Historians. Historical. Archive. Curator. Museums. Artifacts. Fossils. Dinosaurs. Paleontology. Archaeology. Ancient. Interval. Circa. Century. Yuga. Epoch. Eras. Generation. Genealogy. Ancestry. Lineage. Elders. Old age. Aging. Heirloom. Antiques. Relic. Vintage. Retro. Previous. Former. Landmark. Monument. Memorial. Commemorate. Reminisce. Memento. Keepsake. Souvenir. Collectors. Collection. Pack rats. Clutter. Junk. Absence. Absent. Juvenile. Childish. Pigtails. Bow tie. Stature. Height. Tall. Short. Small. Tiny. Little. Diminutive. Mini. Miniature. Munchkin.

Underage. Outgrow. Quaint. Postpone. Stalling. Delays. Tardy. Late. Overdue. Rain check. Lag. Stale. Expired. Out of date. Old fashioned. Antiquated. Archaic. Extinct. Prehistoric. Antiquity. Dust. Musty. Rusty. Irrespon sible. Wrinkles.

47 (Seven of Cups) Famous. Name & fame. Notoriety. Renown. Name recognition. (Inter)nationally known. High profile. VIP. Well-known. Household name. Public life. Limelight. Legendary. Notable. Noteworthy. Eminent. Prominent. Marquee. Honorary. Legacy. The future. Tomorrow. Foresight. Visionary. Clairvoyance. Futurist. Prognosticate. Predictions. F orecast. Meteorology. Picks. Selection. Candidate. Nominee. Modern. Modernize. Pantheon. Ballad. Daydreaming. Shallow. Superficial. Surface. Infamy. Notorious.

48 (Eight of Cups) Purpose. Meaning. Mission. Direction. Destination. Guidance. Goals. Aims. Worthwhil e. Quest. Journey. Tour. Traveler. Tourist. Visitor. Path. Way. Road trip. On the road. Road map. Navigate. GPS. Location. Where. Trucks. Semis. Rigs. Convoy. Caravan. Rock 'n roll. Rock concert. Bass. Tribute. Adore. Euphoria. Returning. Nomad. Wandering. Sky. Heaven. Reme mbering God. Worship. Renunciation. Monastic. Pilgrimages. Bhakti yoga. Sadhaka. Chanting. Seeking & finding. Forgetting & remembering. Reminder(s). Recollection. Unattached. Leave. Abandonment. Stranded. Lost. Meander. Wandering aimlessly. Errant. Disillusionment. Wasting time. Dropout. Slacker. Loafer. Hollow.

49 (Nine of Cups) Happiness. Fulfillment. Satisfaction. Contentment. Santosh. Satiety. Wish fulfillment. Delight. Gratification. Yes. Smiling. Fruit. Citrus. Berries. Jelly. Jam. Seeds. Ho ney. Sweets. Sugar. Stevia. Soda. Snacks. Dessert. Toppings. Caramel. Fudge. Chocolate. Co coa. Syrup. Treats. Candy. Candy bar. Cookies. Doughnuts. Pie. Cake. Cupcakes. Frosting. Icing. Glaze. Confection. Sweetness. Sweetheart. Sweetie. Sauces. Dips. Chips. Pizza. Indulgence. Full. Piano. Yoga. Pancreas. Si ckeningly sweet. Sassy. Self-satisfied. Smug.

50 (Ten of Cups) Family life. Ananda. Bliss. Joy. Overjoyed. Wonderful. World peace. Global. Worldwide. Planetary. Planet. Earth. World. Gaia. Globe. Continent. Culture. Society. Population. Civilization. World family. Everyone. We. Symphony. Orchestra. Chorus. Conductor. Composer. Opera. Sonata. Social issues. Nonviolence. Sociology. Environment. Conservation. Steward. Stewardship. Land. Re al

estate. Habitat. Wilderness. Forest. Wildlife. Botany. Plants. Biology. Ecology. Climate. Bios
phere. Ocean. Sea. Maritime. Marine life. Sea life. Whales. Seals. Dolphins. Coast
Guard. Rainbow. Rainfall. Downpour. Drench. Torrential. Floods. Deluge. Ark. Tidal
waves. Tsunami. Earthquakes. Natural disasters. Mudslides. World war. Cataclysm.

51 (King of Swords) Right
life. Swadharma. Truth. Honesty. Honor. Respect. Integrity. Character. Reputation. Admirati
on. Credentials. Veracity. Virtue. Ethics. Morals. Honor. Dignity. Decency. Conduct. Behavio
r. Authority. Legislation. Laws. Rules. Regulations. Ordinance. Policy. Standards. Criterion.
Important. Significant. Appropriate. Formal. Official. Proper. Salute. Sir. Citizen. Civilian. C
ampaign. Elections. Voting. Inauguration. Politics. Govern. Government. The
State. Mayor. Governor. Lawmakers. Legislature. Congress. President. Pentagon. Military. G
enerals. Soldiers. Troops. Infantry. Armed Forces. Police. Law
enforcement. Sheriff. Marshall. Officer. Jurisdiction. Lawyers. Attorneys. Legal
advice. Counsel. Litigation. Lawsuit. (Un)constitutional. Evidence. Proof. Ammunition. Mast
ermind. Genius. Logic. Rational. Factual. Accurate. Exact. Precise. Frankness. Candor. Brief.
Plain
spoken. Objective. Impartial. Unbiased. Serious. Sober. Solemn. Gravitas. Formidable. Accre
ditation. Instructor. Instruction
manual. Textbook. Instructions. Lessons. Procedure. Automate. Computerize. Computers. M
achines. Linear. Methodical. Systematic. Statistics. Facts. What. Arithmetic. Math. Equation.
Formulas. Quotient. Enumerate. Naming. Numerology. Counting. Quantify. Measurements.
Parameter. Calibrate. Requirements. Qualifications. License. Permits. Legitimate. Liturgy. Ch
aplain. Salute. Blunt. Deadpan. Disciplinarian. Authoritarian. Bureaucracy. Disclaimer. Legal
ese. Legalistic. Rule-
bound. Stickler. Exacting. Stringent. Rigorous. Strict. Stern. Severe. Draconian. Inhibitions.
Repression. Rigid. Intimidate. Adversary. Dour. Harsh. Mean. Cruel. Merciless. Relentless.
Brutal. Cold. Unfeeling. Unemotional. Callous. Desensitized. Dehumanize. Mechanical. Robot
ic. Automaton. Armor. Weapons. Gunsmith. Swordsmanship. Euthanasia.

52 (Queen of
Swords) Keen. Perceptive. Astute. Shrewd. Incisive. Wit. Verbose. Analyze. Why. How. Expl
ain. Astrology. Horoscope. Midpoints. Critique. Criticism. Sarcasm. Satire. Snarky. Snide. S
harp tongue. Smart
mouth. Wisecrack. Comebacks. Invective. Scathing. Caustic. Corrosive. Skewer. Lampoon. G
ossip. Rumors. Tabloids. Justifications. Rationalizations. Mask
cutter. Ultimatums. Patronizing. Condescending. Sanctimonious. Scorn. Cynical. Hypocrite.
Contradiction. Manipulative. Homewrecker. Smack. Catty. Insults. Put
downs. Faultfinding. Nag. Hag. Crone. Emasculate. Stiletto. Cackle. Shrill. Shrieking. Shrew.

Spinster. Widow. Cobwebs. Arachnids. Arachne. Weave. Tapestry. High maintenance. Warts. Bitter. Cruella. Dream-wrecker.

53 (Knight of Swords) Forthright. Straightforward. Discussion. Debating. Offense. Principles. Scruples. Cre ed. Doctrine. Persuade. Convince. Compelling. Warrior. Crusader. Evangelist. Preacher. Prea ching. Sermon. Homily. Ministry. Missionary. Converting. Theology. Religionist. bible. Gosp el. Testament. Profess. Pontificate. Proselytizing. Indoctrinate. Dogma. Beliefs. Opinions. Co nfrontational. Conflict. Dispute. Argue. Combative. Attacking. Dissuade. Discourage. Disarm. Cheap shots.

54 (Page of Swords) Spontaneous. Curious. Inquisitive. Interesting. Fascinating. Conversational. Ingeniou s. Clever. Quick thinking. Scout. Intelligence gathering. Surveillance. Confirm. Confirmation. Corroborate. Onlooker. Witness. Observe. Vi ew. Watch. Oversee. Overlook. Overhear. Listen. Ears. Audiotape. Videotape. Recording. Fo otage. Scan. Snippet. Videographer. Inquire. Interview. Interrogate. Questions. Polls. Trivia. Riddles. Puzzles. Crossword puzzles. Quiz. Questionnaire. Querent. Discussion. Forums. Laboratory. Research. Experime nt. Microscope. Lens. Specimen. Sample. Documentation. Factors. Congruence. Correlation. Estimate. Guess. Conjecture. Theory. Postulate. Assumption. Clues. Fingerprints. Geminian. Mind reading. Telepathy. Teleport. Memorize. Verbatim. Quote. Recite. Extemporaneous. Improvis ation. Demonstrate. Examples. Exhibit. Display. Silicon. Engineer. Programming. Technology . Internet. Online. Website. .com Interface. Simulation. Virtual. Cyber. Digital. Monitor. Scr een. Graphics. Pixels. Frame. Cover. Holographic. 3D. Transparency. Superimpose. Phase. T echnical. Applications. Software. Version. Modify. Upgrades. Enhancements. Characteristics. Identity. Alias. Screen name. Avatar. Profile. Video. Download. Upload. Sensor. Stimuli. Dashboard. Vicarious. Sha peshifting. Chameleon. Birds. Mockingbird. Parrot. Copy. Imitate. Impersonate. Impression. Mimic. Photocopy. Duplicate. Double. Twins. Split. Bifurcate. Dual. Multiple. Poly. Replicate . Simultaneous. Exponential. Who. Similar. Resemble. Portray. Cameo. Audition. Role. Role playing. Repertoire. Juxtapose. Transcribe. Dialogue. Narrate. Documentary. Recital. Fluency . Conversant. Language. Bilingual. Multilingual. Interpret. Translator. Accent. Dialects. Ling o. Approximate. Ditto. Crossover. Pause. Karaoke. Sing-along. Dubbing. Voice overs. Make over. Masks. Disguise. Camouflage. Costumes. A prop. Gesture. Parody. Spoof. Mock. Skit. Charade. Irony. Wink. Mannequin. Breezy. Windy . Horses. Pony. Confidant. Spy. Infiltrate. Insider. Undercover. Covert. Secret agent. Incognito. Debrief. (De)code. Decipher. Uncover. Expose. Erase. Delete. Data. Encode . Passwords. Secret

codes. Encryption. Documents. Files. Memoir. Autobiography. Distraction. Tangent. Coy. Cu nning. Outsmart. Replacement. Pretender. Poseur. Impostor. Copycat. Replica. Unravel. Lay ers. Veneer. Facade. Nosy. Snitch. Tattle tale. Fink. Informant. Leak. Filter. Revise. Restore. Reverse. Janus. Two-faced. Flip-flopper. Ping pong. Fickle. Raw. Peel. Disrobe. Bare. Nude. Exhibitionist. Peek. Peephole. Kinky. Deviate. Double cross. Doublespeak. Double meaning. Double entendre. Duplicity. Mixed messages. Boggle. Bewilder. Conundrum. Rhetoric. Pun. Idiom. Binoculars. Double vision. Blurry. Vague. Impersonal. Laminate. Cellophane. Plastic. Artificial. Synthetic. Polym er. Cellular. DNA. Genetics. Genes. Traits. Genome. Chromosome. Sequence. Hybrid. Clone. Meddle. Tamper. Intrude. Eavesdropping. Wiretapping. Reconnaissance. Scrutiny. Mockum entary. Counterintelligence. Brainwash. Misinformation. Disinformation. Misrepresent. Plagia rize. Allegedly. Ambidextrous. Switch hitter. Hermaphrodite. Androgyny. Gender identity. Unisex. Outed. Geek. Eccentric. Elastic. Plasticity. Augmentation. Silicone. Prosthes is. Bionics. Cyborg. Doppelganger.

55 (Ace of Swords) Insight. Clarity. Brilliance. Reading & writing. Mindfulness. Knowledge. Philosophy. Brainstorming. Cogitate. Words. Delineate. De fine. Definition. Dictionary. Lexicon. Vocabulary. Spelling. Alphabet. Letters. Encyclopedia. Reference. Answers. Solutions. Problem solving. Proprietary. Patent. Copyright. Publisher. Editor. Writer. Author. Wordsmith. Treati se. Essays. Books. Manuscript. Screenplay. Plays. Novels. Contents. Text. Inscription. Print. Script. Cursive. Handwriting. Legibility. Paper. Typing. Typewriter. Hard copy. Literacy. Comprehension. Cognition. Intellect. Intelligence. The mind. The brain. Cerebral. Synapse. Thoughts. Ideas. Notion. Differentiate. Discernment. (In)correct. R ight/wrong. Clear. Perception. Realizations. Brainpower. Strong mind. Open-minded. Broad-minded. Freethinker. Mind-blowing. Upavasana. Fasting. Open-eyed. Light bulb. Lumens. Pithy. Scribble. Mentality. Ideology. Absolute. Supremacy. Ethnicity. Narrow-minded. Prejudice. Segregate.

56 (Two of Swords) Decisive. Choosing. Selecting. Decisions. Maybe. Serenity. Diplomacy. Ambassador. Peacemaking. Negotiate. Compromise. Settlement. Conciliatory. Mediate. Cease fire. Neutral. Equilibrium. Customer service. Polite. Agreeable. Agreement. Accommodate. Poise. Composure. Tact. Graceful. Con genial. Civility. Etiquette. Libran. Ambivalent. Delicate. Truce. Treaty. Accord. Pact. Pacify. Tiebreaker. Tie. Stalemate. A draw. Standoff. Non-answers. Dithering.

57 (Three of Swords) Consoling. Solace. Tender hearted. Heartthrob. Heartbeat. Condolences. Heartbreaker. Heartache. Tearjerker. Tears. Te

ar drops. Crying. Weeping. Loneliness. Lonesome. Sadness. Broken
hearted. Separations. Whining. Self-pity.

58 (Four of Swords) Wellness. Well being. Bodily health. Healthy body. Robust health. Strong
constitution. Healthful. Hardy. Moose. Rest. Relaxation. Respite. Hotel. Vacation. Staycation
. Time out. Intermission. Halftime. Recess. Time
off. Weekend. Sunday. Comeback. Recover. Restore. Recuperate. Nap. Mattress. Bed. Bedti
me. Therapy. Therapist. Physical therapy. Rehabilitation. Herbs. Treatment. Remedy. Safe
place. Sanctuary. Refuge. Retirement. Hut. Forest dweller. Kaya
kalpa. Retreat. Tired. Overworked. Overtime. Patient. Medical. Physician. Doctor. Medic. M
edicine. Medication. Prescription. Pharmacy. Dosage. Side
effects. Chloroform. Anesthesia. Sedation. Hospitals. Ambulances. Stretcher. Gurney. Bed
rest. Infirmary. Convalescence. Disease. Ailment. Ill. Sick. Overdose. Civil
unrest. Ousted. Banishment. Exile. Ostracize. Shunning. Enforced isolation. Quarantine.

59 (Five of
Swords) Savior. Redeemer. Redemption. Messiah. Ascension. Catharsis. Sacrifice. Salvage. A
nchor. Esoteric. Feng
shui. Reiki. Crystals. Baptism. Anoint. Consciousness. Detoxification. Conceding. Defeat. Los
e. Failure. Wreckage. Sink. Scuttle. Underwater. Down. Low. Dredge. Dismantle. Shatter. Pi
eces. Ream. Rip. Tear
apart. Mutilation. Dissect. Eviscerate. Dismember. Butcher. Slaughter. Carnivore. Scourge.
Whip. Persecution. Mithras. Martyr. Crucify. Impale. Fallibility. Scapegoat. Humiliate. Chagr
in. Mudslinging. Demoralize. Empty
victory. Enemy. Deserter. Mutiny. Disgrace. Ashamed. Violated. Disfigure. Neutron. Negativ
e
energy. Atomic. Nuclear. Fission. Radiation. Mutation. Fallout. Radioactive. Toxic. Toxicolog
y. Contaminate. Annihilate. Orange. Allergies. Sneezing. Unsportsmanlike conduct. Game
over. Personal meltdown. Breakdown. Agony. Mayhem. Tempest. Thorn. Self-
interest. Cult. Dredge. Deflate. Funerals.

60 (Six of Swords) Progress. Moving forward. Forward thinking. Thinking ahead. Long
range. Distant. Far away. Long
distances. Departure. Passage. Voyage. Overseas. Abroad. Float. Ferry. Import. Export. Tran
splant. Revolutionize. Fundamentals. Science. Physics. Vedic. Complex. Alternative. Topogra
phy. Geography. Subterranean. Underground. Basement. Cave. Surround. Boundaries. Borde
r. Perimeter. Fence. Sidelines. Domestic. Foreign. Emigration. Immigration. Migration. Exoti
c. Native. Indigenous. Clan. Tribe. Approach. Avoid. Outsider. Counterpoint. Dissent. Zeal.
Fervor. Reform(er). Contrarian. Unique. Asterisk. Anomaly. Outlier. Fluke. Aberration. Unn
atural. Repel. Insects. Bugs. Annoyance. Bother. Irritate. Nuisance. Pesky. Hassles. Peeved.

Inconvenient. Difficult. Refuse. Resist. Defy. Defiant. Contra. Nonconformist. Unorthodox. B reak
away. Schism. Faction. Fringe. Periphery. Marginalized. Alienation. Tribal. Aboriginal. Indig enous. Primitive. Backwards. Misfit. Mutant. Infliction. Backlash. Beasts. Rabid. Extremist. Radical. Guerrilla. Insurgent. Rebel. Rebellion. Insurrection. Uprising. Overthrow. Takeover. Coup
d'etat. Secede. Subversive. Propaganda. Censorship. Regime. Theocracy. Warlord. Transfer. Extradite. Deport. Annul. Irreconcilable differences. Estrangement. Ex. Divorce.

61 (Seven of Swords) Strategy. Planning. Contingency plans. Back up plans. Plan B. Change of plans. Tactics. Stealth. Chess. Exit. Running away. Escape. Flee. Evade. Getting
away. Elusive. Tracking. Follow. Trail. Tracks. Footprints. Tracking. Pursue. Chase. Hunt. H unter. Prey. Pounce. Dodge. Skip. Stray. Missing. Vanish. Disappear. Invisible. Invisibility. Hide. Hidden. Conceal. Drop-
off. Ramp. Slope. Hill. Slalom. Bobsled. Sled. Luge. Toboggan. Slick. Slippery. Lubrication. Hips. Shirk. Guile. Trick. Trickster. Subterfuge. Hoodie. Tiptoe. Furtive. Sneaky. Shady. Sch eme. Fraudulence. Foil. Cheating. Rogue. Lone
wolf. Wolves. Coyote. Wily. Disloyal. Bandit. Rip
off. Pilfer. Heist. Theft. Stolen. Shoplfting. Robbery. Burglary. Break-
in. Intruder. Abscond. Fugitive. Poacher. Lurk. Ambush.

62 (Eight of
Swords) Access. Entrance. Entry. Password. Unauthorized. Restrictions. Limitations. Obstruc tions. Impediments. Blockage. Blockade. Barrier. Barricade. Barred. Prohibit. Ban. Hockey. Suspensions. Honk. Horn. Frustrations. Interference. Veto. Block. Thwart. Hinder. Hamperi ng. Impediment. Maze. Labyrinth. Minotaur. Neck. Jaw. Windpipe. Throat. Larynx. Esopha gus. Gullet. Swallow. Tongue. Bite. Unpopularity. Booing. Eliminate. Bathroom. Toilet. Fece s. Flush. Plumber. Plumbing. Plunger. (Un)clog. Sewer. Drains. Pipe. Tether. Bracelet. Cord . Cables. Elevator. Gatekeeper. Gate. Knock. Bang. Doorbell. Doors. Keys. Locks. Locksmith. (Un)lock. Open. Close. Release. Detain. Arrest. Apprehend. Capture. Caught. Handcuff. Co nfinement. Victim. Suspect. Criminal. Convict. Prisoner. Jail. Jailer. Contain(ment). Lockdo wn. Contraband. Walls. Wall
off. Cage. Captive. Captivity. Jailbreak. Hacking. Net. Snare. Entangle. Tangled. Binding. Tr apped. Immobile. Narrow. Tighten. Constrict. Snake. Serpentine. Slither. Wrap. Coil. Tail. Rattle. Hiss. Venom. Fangs. Bag. Stuffed. Stuck. Logjam. Gridlock. Impasse. (Un)plug. Cork . A box. Fright. Frighten. The chills. Goose
bumps. Petrify. Moan. Grumble. Groan. Growl. Antisocial. Hostile. Cracks. Laryngitis. Whee ze. Cough. Congestion. Constipation. Leash. Rope. Knot. Slipknot. Noose.

63 (Nine of
Swords) Compassion. Relief. Alleviate. Surgeon. Intestines. If. Concerns. Distress. Worries. Worried
sick. Fretting. Crucial. Critical. Acute. Grief. Grieving. Weeping. Wailing. Lament. Misery. A nguish. Suffering. Woe. Mourn. Nightmares. Pitiful. Desperation. Harrowing. Dire. Emergen cies. Tragic.

64 (Ten of
Swords) Conclusion. Finality. End. Done. Over. Inevitable. Refrigerators. Coolers. Freezers. Defrost. Thaw. Melt. Cold. Chilly. Frosty. Frigid. Freeze. Frozen. Deep freeze. Sub-zero. Ice. Iceberg. Penguin. Glacier. Tundra. Polar. Arctic. Winter. Wintry. Slush. Blizzard. Whiteout. Flurries. Snow. Snowflake. Snowfall. Snowball. Snowman. Igloo. Nordic. Vikings. Dusk. Final chapter. Closing. Indefinitely. Endlessly. Never-ending. Interminable. Never. Last. Final. Finish. Cryogenics. Snowballing. Cascade. Avalanch e. Abominable. Abyss. Abysmal. Glum. Deep sadness. Major depression. Listlessness. Mope. Dreary. Bleak. Bummer. Slump. Tanking. Dismal failure. Misfortune. Backstabbing. Finished. Ruin. Demise.

65 (King of Pentacles) Worldly success. Business advice. Calculating. Big business. Corporate. CEO. The big boss. Tycoon. Mogul. Magnate. Center of power. Empires. Kingdom. Unions. Contracts. Economy. Economics. Macroeconomics. Finan ce. Financing. Treasurer. Bankers. Banks. Vaults. Mining. Gold. Silver. Platinum. Bullion. G ems. Jewels. Jewelry. Jeweler. Lapidary. Diamonds. Facet. Sparkle. Glitter. Treasure. Pricele ss. Precious. Rare. Kingmaker. Influence. Clout. Linchpin. Bankroll. Corporations. Backroom deals. Lobbying. Monopolies. Cartels. Whistleblower. Nicknames. Bling. Big bucks. Casinos. High roller. Gambling. Speculation. Wager. Bet. Blackjack. Playing poker. Bluffing. Roulette. Billiards. Limousine. Chauffeur. Top hat. Penthouse. Playboy. Cigars. Nightclub. Disco. Hip-hop. Rap. Urban. Mix. Turf. Territory. Nose ring. Filthy rich. Fat cat. Hog. Spit. Garish. Tasteless. Crude. Vulgar. Ribald. Base. Vile. Nasty. Gross. Lowbrow.

Explicit. Smut. Blackmail. Shakedown. Extortion. Bribery. Kickbacks. Underhanded. Graffiti.

Taggers. Vandalism. Hustler. Vice. Corruption. Graft. Crony. Mob. Syndicate. Kingpin. Thug gery. Hooligan. Swearing. Cussing. Expletives. Bullsh*t. Vomit. Barf. Nausea. Lousy. Olfacto ry. Odor. Smell.

66 (Queen of Pentacles) Managing money. Microeconomics. Benefits. Benefits package. Nest egg. Pension. 401k. 403b. IRA's. Cd's (certificates of deposit). Mutual funds. Money

market. Stocks. Bonds. Investments. Portfolios. Annuities. Dividends. Severance packages. Bacon. Sausage. Pork. Gold digger. Suspicious. Hippie.

67 (Knight of Pentacles) Stability. Reliability. Dependability. Grihastha. Householder. Home owner. Homemaker. Housework. Household tasks. Laundry. Yard work. Toil. Taurian. Average person. Average day. Daily life. Ordinary. Common. Regular. Average. Normal. Usual. Consistent. Turtle. Tortoise. Mundane. Sudra. Plodding. Lazy. Sloth. Sedentary. Sluggish. Couch potato. Dullard. Drone. Tedious. Monotony. Slob.

68 (Page of Pentacles) Learning. Studying. Education. Student. Pupil. School. College. University. Campus. Scholar. Academic. Academia. Library. Educated. Well learned. Book smart. Graduate. Tutor. Professor. Educator. Lettered. PhD. Highly educated. Seminar. Curriculum. Syllabus. Courses. Classes. Desk. Grades. GPA. Homework. Research. Tenure. School funding. Educational grants. Student grants. Scholarships. Tuition. Pundit. Domesticated. House broken. Tame. Pedigree. Protests. Student protests.

69 (Ace of Pentacles) Income. Earnings. Salary. Pay. Revenue. Earning potential. Payday. Deposits. Withdrawals. Assets. Resources. Resourcefulness. Practicality. Affordability. Acquire. Own. Valuable. Expensive. Fancy. Fine. Classy. Snazzy. Sharp dresser. Creature comforts. Easy living. Teflon coating. Easy money. Monetary incentive. Economic incentive. Expenses. Liabilities. IRS.

70 (Two of Pentacles) Flexibility. Handling change. Multi-tasking. Juggling. Coping. Budgeting. Accounting. Financial records. Bookkeeping. Accountants. CPA's. Audits. Fluctuations. Contortionists.

71 (Three of Pentacles) Professional. Quality work. Good work. Craftsmanship. Well made. Custom made. Customized. Skilled labor. Skilled trade. Profession. Vocation. Artisan. Handicraft. Merit. Quality. Excellence. Masterpiece. Inspiring work. Impressive. Mediocre. So-so. Shoddy. Botched.

72 (Four of Pentacles) Frugal. Thrifty. Economical. Financially conservative. Millionaire mind. Holding firm. Traditional. Conventional. Savings. Cheap. Avarice. Greedy. Hoard. Scrimp. Miserly. Stingy. Scrooge. Tightwad. Penny pincher. Cheapskate.

73 (Five of Pentacles) Employment. Job. Occupation. Workplace. Hiring. Human Resources. Personnel. Compensation. Shelter. Housing. Roof. Temporary. Capable. Made. Maker. Cobble. Project. Able-bodied. Tapas. Austerities. Ascetic. Hunger. Deprivation. Poverty. Impoverished. Penniless. Indigent. Lack. Jalopy. Dilapidated. Eject. Eviction. Homeless. Beggars. Destitute. Limbs. Crutches. Disability. Handicap. Dumpster. Dispose. Trash. Garbage. Rubbish. Debris. Discard. Disposable. Laid off. Downsizing. Recession. Disabled. Incapable. Emaciated. Famine.

74 (Six of Pentacles) Sharing. Generosity. Giving. Gifts. Charity. Philanthropy. Contribute. Benefactors. Donors. Donations. Offerings. Contributions. Funding. Fund-raiser. Fund-raising. Recipient. Bestow. Regifting. Ribbon. Bow. Racy. Entitlements. Handouts.

75 (Seven of Pentacles) Patience. Calming down. Anticipation. Harvest. Squirrel. Altered states. Zany. Self-diagnosis. Symptom. Procrastination. Impatience. Hesitate. Anxiety. Paranoia. Panic. Phobia. Neurosis.

76 (Eight of Pentacles) Efficiency. Productivity. Industriousness. Apprenticeship. Workshop. Manufacture. Factories. Industry. Assembly lines. Production. Mass produce. Streamline. Processed. Franchise. Homogenous. Monoculture. Detours. Shortcuts. Cutoff. Cutting corners. Jaywalking. Forge. Trespassing.

77 (Nine of Pentacles) Prayer. Affluence. Independently wealthy. Well-to-do. Elite. Superior. Refined. Sophisticated. Aristocrat. Nobility. Socialite. Posh. Pretentious. Snob. Stuck up. Snooty.

78 (Ten of Pentacles) Being wealthy. Vast family wealth. Generational wealth. Artha. Dynasty. Manifesting.

This is a list of **sayings and multiple word descriptions** for the numbers **23 to 78**. Again, for the numbers 23 through 78 the corresponding tarot card follows the number in parentheses.

23 (King of Wands) Just do it! Leading the way. Taking the lead. Leader of the pack. A real go-getter. Physical activity. Being your own boss.

24 (Queen of Wands) My body is a temple. Cleaning house. Cleaning up your act. Getting cleaned up. Pure and natural. Go organic. Eating healthy. Food safety. Chew your food. Brushing your teeth. Dental hygiene. Pearly whites. Taking charge. Who's in charge here? I'm in charge. The power behind the throne. Take the vow. Saving it for marriage. Put some clothes on. Keep your clothes on. Wearing the pants in the family. Ruling the roost. Ruling with an iron fist. Chew on this. Food allergies. Tap out. Bow out. The emperor has no clothes.

25 (Knight of Wands) On the go. Adventures are to the adventurous. Rooting for the underdog. Change of residence. Not in one place for long. Can't sit still. Having to change location.

26 (Page of Wands) Let's talk. Call me. Pep talk. Good looks. Looking good. Beauty draws more than oxen. A bird with a beautiful plumage doesn't sit in the corner. Look at me. The face came before the photograph. A picture is worth a thousand words. Good call. Good news. Good press. Those who bring good news knock hard. No news is good news. News reports. In the news. Multimedia journalist. Post office. Postage stamps. Bad news.

27 (Ace of Wands) Take the initiative. Taking the first step. Get started. Getting started. Start it up. It's a start. Turning over a new leaf. No harm in trying. Do what you will, but be the first. Brand new. New and improved. On your mark, get set, GO! "And they're off..." Off and running. All talk and no action. Short-lived bursts of extreme enthusiasm. Overly enthusiastic. Gung ho. Exclamation point. Acting out of character. Not being yourself. Jumping the gun. False start. False alarms. False positive. This is only a drill.

28 (Two of Wands) Be bold. Be daring. Here I come to save the day. Where there's a will there's a way. Overcoming all obstacles. Making the impossible possible. Nothing is impossible. I will do what I will to do. Fortune favors the bold. Only the strong survive. Flexing your muscles. Not living up to your full potential.

29 (Three of Wands) Cooperate. Joining forces. Teaming up. There's no "I" in team. TEAM: together each accomplishes more. Confident in your abilities. Honing your skills and talents. Consult an expert. A team of experts.

30 (Four of Wands) Count your blessings (lest they flee). You have a lot to be thankful for. Quality of life. Home sweet home. Thank you. Praise the Lord. Fashion sense. Best dressed. Sense of style. Living a life of luxury. Better Homes and Gardens. Tennis court. No-fuss. Born with a silver spoon in your mouth. Thanks but no thanks. Perpetually offended. You don't know what you've got 'til it's gone. To take for granted.

31 (Five of Wands) Striving to be number 1. Personal best. Outdoing yourself. Rising to the challenge. Strive and thrive. Stirring things up. Stirring the pot. Shake it up. Provoke a reaction. Getting a rise out of someone. Raising a ruckus. Things get out of hand. Prove you wrong. I'll show you. In your face. Bring it on. C'mon. Go for it. Risking it all. Here comes trouble. It takes two to make a quarrel. Stepping into the ring. Throwing your hat into the ring. Getting into the mix. Laying it on the line. Leveling the playing field. On your own terms. Mixed martial arts. Hard struggle for material existence. Out of spite. Getting your goat. I can't compete with you. Working at cross purposes. Disorderly conduct. Riot starter. Anything goes. Free-for-all.

32 (Six of Wands) You win. Middle of the road. One size fits all. One stop shopping. Knock it out of the park. Hitting a home run. Record setting. Award-winning. Bigger is better. Mighty giant. Larger than life. Over the top. Keep it simple. Ease of use. Love of one's country. Majority rules. Reign/rule. Self-sufficiency. Climate control. Air conditioning. Fast food. Must have. Gotta have it. I want it all and I want it now. Instant gratification. Immediate self-gratification. The short-term. Short attention span. Taking the path of least resistance. Taking the easy way out. Any excuse is better than none. Telling you what to do. I'll do what I want to do. Rugged individualism. Freedom march. Baseball bat. Swing batter batter swing. Packing a punch. Cushion the blow. I'm not going down without a fight. It takes two blows to make a battle. The first blow does not hurt like the second. Your liberty ends where my nose begins. A kick in the butt. Pick on someone your own size. Picking a fight. Put up your dukes. Duking it out. Body blow. Living well beyond your means.

33 (Seven of Wands) Be brave. Be courageous. Taking a stand. Standing up for yourself. Standing your ground. Standing firm. Stand with us or stand aside. That takes a lot of guts. Having a strong backbone. The small of the back. Not backing down. Not caving in. Not letting people walk all over you. Red badge of courage. Defending the championship. Regaining/retaining the title. Putting on a good show. Big hat, no cattle. A big talker. Into the lion's den. Fraidy cat.

34 (Eight of Wands) Go at the right speed. Strike while the iron's hot. Get it while it's hot. Things happen really quickly. Don't rush. Pace yourself. Haste makes waste. Speed up. Slow down. Hitting the brakes. Slow your roll. Full throttle. Full tilt. Full speed ahead. Pedal to the metal. Top speed. Motorized vehicle. Car & driver. Race car driver. Race track. Pace car. High speed. High octane. Where the rubber meets the road. Road racing. Drag race. Hot rod. Wanna ride? Pick up the pace. Speedy delivery. Rush hour traffic. High-speed rail. Bullet train. Faster than a speeding bullet. Fast moving. Energy in motion. F=MA (force = mass times acceleration). Quick action. Slower/faster. Hot shot. Don't stress. Don't stress out over it. Blowing off steam. Burn off some energy. Going for a run. Running laps. Cooling off. Cooling down. IM (instant message). Urgent message. Fast blast. Back-to-back. How often? Wired up. Fired up. Warm up. Turning up the heat. That's hot. Throwing gas on the fire. Fanning the flames. Spreading like wild fire. Motorized fan. Circulate air. Getting all fired up. Generating a buzz. Ratings spike. Hot sauce. Hot chili peppers. That's hot. Smokin' hot. Red-hot. Piping hot. Hot tub. Hot water. Boiling hot. Pressure cooker. Natural gas. Blast furnace. Radiant heat. Heating element. Hot air balloon. Out of the frying pan and into the fire. If you play with fire you will get burned. If you can't stand the heat, then get out of the kitchen. Several irons in the fire. Fire-engine red. Fire extinguisher. Blowing out the candles. Billowing smoke. Where there's smoke there's fire. A fire in the heart makes smoke in the head. Flare up. Hot spots. Fire in the hole. Blowing your top/stack. That burns me up. Strike a flint and you get fire. Light my fire. Fueling the fire. Tinder box. The one who strikes first, strikes twice. Hitting a moving target. Burning your candle at both ends. Ain't slowing down. Full tank of gas. Run out of gas. Empty tank. Running out of steam. Running on empty. Running on fumes. Put a lid on it. Cool it. Wind up. Wound up. Pent up. Bottled up. Stir crazy. Heating up. Burning inside. Rise in temperature. Burning up with fever. Rapid rise. Blood pressure. Rapid pulse. Circulatory system. Cardiovascular system. Shot in the arm. Fleet of foot. Rushing around. In a rush. I can't keep up with you. To go faster, slow down. Festina lente (make haste slowly). The need for speed. Life in the fast lane. Balls to the wall. Going balls out. Firing all the arrows in your quiver. Bow and arrow. Set in motion. Forward momentum. Rise up. Blast off. Jet propulsion. Forward thrust. G-force. Planes, trains, and automobiles. Parking spot/space/lot. Run into the ground. Driving it 'til the wheels fall off. One foot on the gas and one foot on the brakes. Spinning your wheels. Squealing your tires. Burning rubber. Revving your engine. Crash & burn. On fire. First strike. Quick strike. Communication difficulties. Wires crossed. Circuit breaker. Stressed out. Nerve wracking. Frayed nerves. Striking a nerve. Raw nerve. Burn out. Coffee & cigarettes. Nic fits. Skin conditions. In flames. Powder keg. Short fuse. Tempers flare. Going berserk. Lashing out in anger. Angry outbursts. Boiling mad. Reptilian brain.

35 (Nine of Wands) Persevere. Be alert. Be prepared. Getting ready. Forewarned is forearmed. Defending yourself. Hang in there. The long haul. Strength in adversity. Strength in reserve. Staying power. Track & field. Cross-country. Keep on going. Keep on doing what you're

doing. Stick with it. Never give up. Not giving up. Don't quit. Don't stop. So far, so good. Don't switch horses midstream. Staying the course. Keep it up. In it for the duration. On an even keel. Sticking to you like glue. If you're in love then nothing else matters, if you're not in love then nothing else matters. To be continued. Fire-resistant. Fire-retardant. A real lifesaver. Life preserver. I've got your back. Leave it to me. Limited term insurance. Term life insurance. Effective immediately. Red alert. Heads up. Head wound. Being caught off guard. On guard! It's better to warn than to be warned. They that get the next best are not ill off. It's easy to hold the fort when it's not attacked. Stick around. Hang around. Longest lasting. Going the distance. Keeps going and going. On and on. I get knocked down, but I get up again. An ounce of prevention is worth a pound of cure. Just in case. Shake it off. Bounce back. Temporary setback. Stuck between a rock and a hard place. Stop interrupting me. Wearing me out. I'm worn out. Bare bones. Been through hell and back. Taking a toll. A temp. Cutting it short. Threatening to quit. Calling it quits. I quit. I give up. I can't go on. Throwing in the towel. Give up (on). Cut short. That didn't last long. Letting your guard down. On your last legs. Life threatening. Keel over.

36 (Ten of Wands) Unburden yourself. Lighten your load. I can handle it. Working hard and being responsible for yourself. Height of achievement. Elevated to new heights. Rising to great heights. The goal is in sight. Step by step. Getting out of debt. Chipping away at it. Digging out. Getting out from underneath it. Having a weight lifted off of your shoulders. Weight load. Maximum load. Loading up. Weight-bearing exercise. Atlas stones. Hard rocks. Power stairs. Hand grips. Grip strength. Bench press. Upper back. Broad shoulders. Shoulder presses. Overhead press. Lift/raise above your head. Carry you on my shoulders. Shouldering a heavy burden. Feeling like the weight of the world is on your shoulders. There's a lot to unpack there. Only pack what you can carry. Pressing onward. Shrugging your shoulders. Bending over backwards. Doing backflips. Range of motion. Wear a helmet. Strap it on. Adjustable strap. In-line skating. Dig it. In the trenches. Base camp. Rock climbing. Reaching the mountaintop. Rocky Mountain high. Mountain range. Highest mountaintops. Mount Everest. Mount Olympus. Mountain ridge. Mountain peaks. Peaks and valleys. Moving mountains. Upper deck. Drawing the line. Knowing where to draw the line. You've got to draw the line somewhere. Try not to go over the line. Draft horse. Push, pull, drag. It's easier to throw the load off the cart than to put it on. Carry on your back. Falling squarely on your shoulders. It's all you. Personal responsibility. Taking full responsibility. The buck stops here. It's completely up to you. Rise above it. Step it up. Step things up. Taking things to a whole new level. Raising the bar. Fully apply yourself. Heaping on responsibilities. Can you handle this? Handling more than you are expected to handle. Difficult undertaking. Herculean task. Overwhelming task. Heavy lifting. Labors of Hercules. When push comes to shove. Pushing yourself beyond physical limits. Overextending oneself. Maxing out. To the max. Critical mass. Having to cut back. Packing your bags. Exceeding the maximum weight load. Light burden's heavy if far borne. The straw that broke the camel's back. Get the monkey

off your back. Monkey on your back. Overhead bin. Bolt down. Heavy equipment. Heavy earthmoving machinery. Leaving no stone unturned. Weighs a ton. Like a ton of bricks. Cover with a heavy rock. Making a mountain out of a molehill. Twist into knots. Buried in work. Having a lot on your plate. Having your plate full. Having your work cut out for you. Have to do. Mountain of work to do. Total work done. Trying to get someone else to do your work. Come to grips with. Having big shoes to fill. Doing what no one else will do. Demanding a raise. You owe me one. I owe you. Putting you deeper in debt. Going over your credit limit. Over limit. Through the roof. Raising the roof. Raising the debt ceiling. Defaulting on your debt. I'm not paying. Passing the buck. Beast of burden. How much can you lift/carry/bear? More than you bargained for. Out of reach. Full-court press. Rise above oppression. Busting some heads. Like a bull in a china shop. Having a chip on your shoulder. Throwing your weight around. Shoving match. Abuse of power. Excessive force. Going overboard. Going to excessive lengths. Going too far. Raising things to a whole new level. Pushing the limits. Pushing things to the breaking point. Pushed to the brink. Pushed to the limit. To the max. Flip over. Tip over. Tipping point. The last straw. Crossing the line. Going over the line. Beyond the limit. Term limits. Folding the tent. Grinding to a halt. Things slow to a crawl. Brace yourself. Bearing down. Hunkering down. Batten down the hatches. Bearing the brunt of it. Overwhelming force. Under siege. Bringing down the roof. Land on your head. Get a grip. Take a hike. Going over the cliff.

37 (King of Cups) Heart-centered leader. A real family person. Just looking out for your best interest. Wanting the best for you. What comes from the heart goes to the heart. Heart goes where love flows. Matters of the heart. Having a good heart. Pulling at your heart strings. Pouring your heart out. Singing your heart out. Musical instruments. Guitar strum. Sing me a song, you're a singer. Singing in the shower. Having a good voice. Emotional range. Head of the household. Parental guidance. My fellow countrymen. Marine corps. Unit, corps, God, country. Doing it for your country. Swimming pools. Catch the wave. Ride the wave. Burst your bubble. Who's your daddy? Playing the field. A real player. Double dealing. There are plenty of fish in the sea. Liquid of life. It is the water in which we swim. Popping the top. Have a drink. Drinking a little too much is drinking a great deal too much. A red-nosed man may not be a drinker, but he will find nobody to believe it. Slurred speech. In the bottle. Drunk tank. Like a fish out of water. Mixed emotions. The human heart in conflict with itself. Emotional roller coaster. Emotional wreck. On-again, off-again relationships. Love/hate relationships. Double dealing. A player. Tank top. Domestic disputes.

38 (Queen of Cups) Take care. Hold me. Hold me in your arms. Wrap your arms around me. Reach out and touch someone. With arms wide open. Teddy bear. Bear hug. Teddy bear. Sense of touch. Going with your gut. Having a gut feeling. Reflection of feeling. Hooked on a feeling. Feathering a nest. The baby who does not cry does not get fed. Come to mama. Stay at home mom. Touchy feely. Women who care too much. Grin and bear it. Put up

with. Fed up. Clamming up. Milk carton. You're being a big baby. Baby talk. Gaa gaa, goo goo. Fetal position. Self-soothing. I don't care. Don't touch me. Not taking abuse.

39 (Knight of Cups) Be real. The real deal. The real McCoy. Keeping it real. Say kind words to hear kind words. Romantic love. Prince Charming. Dream date. Knight in shining armor. Lover boy. Puppy love. That's nice. Well meaning. With the best of intentions. Keep your promises. Dream come true. Cinderella story. If it sounds too good to be true, it probably is. Living in a dream world. Being a tease. On bended knee. Goody two shoes. The story is only half told when one side tells it. Promise is a bridge of words unsafe to walk across. Seldom is any splendid story wholly true. Holy Grail. Putting someone on a pedestal. Currying favor. Earning brownie points. Saying what you want to hear. Shining you on. Confused love life. In love with a fairytale. Once upon a time...

40 (Page of Cups) Be gentle. How can I help? At your service. Pitching in. Helping out. Doing your part. Doing good works. For the good of my fellow human being. Brotherly love. Brothers and sisters. Good Shepherd. People helping people. Every little helps. The biggest help is help, and even the smallest help is help. Helping build a sense of community. Well tended. To Insure Prompt Service. Public goods. Public services. Social worker. Peer-to-peer. Household staff. Do me a favor. Help me out. Help me. Get some help. Unpaid work. Public assistance. Am I my brother's keeper? The more servants, the worse service. One servant is a servant; two servants are half a servant; three servants are no servants at all. Aid and abet.

41 (Ace of Cups) Melting your heart. Stirrings of the heart. Warming up to you. Open your heart to me. Opening up. Hitting it off. Getting to know one another. Turn me on. About me. If you can't be with the one you love, then love the one you're with. Absence makes the heart grow fonder. Significant difference in age between you and your significant other. Pining away. I just wanna love you. Open relationships. In need of love. Nobody loves me. Sorrow through children. Arrested development. Follow love and it will flee thee; flee love and it will follow thee. Thou shall not covet thy neighbor's wife. Sexual inadequacy. Inhibited sexual desire. Safe sex. Premarital sex. Ménage à trois. Love triangle. A loves B, but B doesn't love A; instead B loves C, so A is crushed. Two-timing. Pro-life / pro-choice. In vitro fertilization. Birth irregularities. Things get ugly. Unwanted sexual contact. Inappropriate sexual contact. Child mistreatment. Menace to society.

42 (Two of Cups) I love you. I love you too. That's beautiful. I do. I now pronounce you man and wife. Two hearts that beat as one. Soul unions. You & I. Just the two of us. Two of a kind. Walking hand in hand. "The one." It takes two to tango. It's a two way street. The feeling is mutual. Love begets love. One thread for the needle, one love for the heart. Lovers have much to relate – but it is always the same thing. Let's hook up. Hook me up. Pucker up. Making out. Sex partners.

43 (Three of Cups) Have fun. Enjoy. Enjoy yourself. "Cheers!" Eat, drink and be merry. The more the merrier. Fun & games. Let's play. Plays well with others. Enjoy it with everyone else. Having a bash. It's party time! Let's party! The life of the party. Make a game out of things. Playing games. Lots of fun. Let's have fun. Are we having fun yet? What do you like to do for fun? Just for kicks. I like that. Let's be friends. Extend the hand of friendship to all you meet. Introduce yourself. Nice to make your acquaintance. Nice to meet you. Greetings and salutations. Hey there. Howdy. Let's meet. Merry meet. Meet and greet. Circle of friends. You're in good company. Having company. Keeping company. Fitting in. At your leisure. Hanging out. Hanging loose. Let loose. Show me a good time. Come out and play. Playing cards. Jump around. Celebratory dance. High fives. Huddle up. To band together. Joining a group. Drawing a crowd. Make 'em laugh. I like a good laugh. Have a good one. Have a nice day. Seasons greetings. Happy holidays. Cheer up. What's for dinner? The horn of plenty. Potluck dinner. Enough is as good as a feast. More fun than a barrel of monkeys. Birds of a feather flock together. Enough is enough. I've had enough. More than enough. The party's over. The fun is over. It's not all fun and games. This is no fun.

44 (Four of Cups) Be here now. Be present. Live in the now. In the present moment. Right here, right now. This is now. How it is. Get used to it. Still here. Here for now. What is. The eternal now. In the zone. Be yourself. Comfortable in your own skin. The skin you're in. I am who I am. I am me. You are you. Just the way you are. Just as I am. It is what it is. I'm alright, right now. Yeah, uh huh. How's it going? What's up? What's going on? What's happening? Here's what's happening. Here's the situation. Assessing the situation. Up-to-date. Status updates. Recently updated. The latest update. Latest development. Keep me up-to-date. I'll keep you posted. Play-by-play. Moment by moment. Current status. Staying current. Stay informed. Staying on topic. Stay tuned. Tune in. Checking in with you to see where you're at with things. Here I am. Crisp and clear. Stream of consciousness. Daily diary. Keeping a log. Short-term memory. Be still. Sitting still. Sit back. Whatever happens, happens. Que será, será. Whatever will be, will be. Accepting things as they are. Let it be. It's all good. The reflexive property: a=a. Small town. Getting into your body. Laid back. Chill out. Zone out. Out of it. Off in your own little world. Out of touch. Can't see yourself. I didn't know that about myself. In denial. Navel-gazing.

45 (Five of Cups) Work your magic. Replace a bad habit with a good one. Common sense is uncommon. Is the glass half empty or half full? Still waters run deep. Do it yourself. If it ain't broke, don't fix it. Educate yourself. Figure it out. Trial and error. Maximum effort. Giving it your all. Giving 110%. All you can do is all you can do. Work smarter – not harder. Working long hours. Investing time and energy. Toughen up. Deep impact. Powerful force. Maximum intensity. Pump up the volume. Go where the energy is. Life-affirming. The school of hard knocks. Personal space. Keep it secret. Why do you ask? That's personal. That's none of your business. Behind closed doors. Private investigator. Deep, dark secrets. See through. X-

ray. Every cloud has a silver lining. Count not what is lost but what is left. Accepting loss. Take away. Tunnel vision. Let it go. What is not. Shades of gray. Like there is a black cloud hanging over your head. You're own your own. Fend for yourself. Life is tough on the streets. Making a mistake. You're being hard on yourself. It's all your fault. Own worst enemy. I feel really bad about that. Suffering in silence. Feel sorry for. That hurts. Ouch. That's gotta hurt. Hard feelings. Hard eyes. Been there, done that. Break the cycle. Kick the habit. I'm hooked. If it happened once, it can happen again. Out of control. Loss of control. The dark side. Coulda, shoulda, woulda. Bitter marriage. The middle finger. Uh oh. I have a bad feeling about this. Spider sense is tingling. Heart sinks. Deep sinking feeling. Things go horribly wrong. Blunt force trauma. expectations > reality = disappointment

46 (Six of Cups) Patiently accept delays. Maintain your innocence. The good ol' days. Golden oldies. Just like old times. For old times sake. For all of history. Making history. History in the making. And the rest is history. A kid at heart. Forever young. The young and the old. April showers bring May flowers. Like clockwork. When the time comes around. On hold. Hold on a minute. You're going to have to wait. I can hardly wait. It's about time. Make/take the time. Don't let time pass you by. Take time to smell the roses. Moment in time. Time capsule. Kids only have one childhood. Coming of age. You're all grown up. The passage of time. Be on time. Don't be late. At the last minute. Better late than never. Let me know when the time comes. Time will tell. Time and date. What time is it? Time clock. Time zones. Daylight savings time. Spring forward, fall back. Turning the clock back. Turning back the hands of time. The shifting sands of time. Cycles of time. Time keeps everything from happening at once. Clocking in and out. There aren't enough hours in the day. Lagging behind. Too late. Too little too late. Due date. Due by. Past due. Are we there yet? Growing pains. Grow up! You're acting like a little kid. Too young. Too old. Growing old. Old-fashioned. Living in the past. Days of old. Back in the day. Taking a walk down memory lane. That's ancient history. Time has passed you by. Get with the times. Dust yourself off. An old man is twice a child. When I was a kid... When I was your age... Back in my day... Old fuddy-duddy.

47 (Seven of Cups) Choosing wisely from among your many options with an eye toward the future. Looking into the future. Vision of the future. Having a bright future. Everybody knows your name. Making a name for yourself. Claim to fame. In the limelight. The one and only. A living legend. Hall of Fame. Leaving a legacy. Say my name. I want to see my name in lights. Fifteen minutes of fame. Name-dropping. Being famous for being famous. I've never heard of 'em. It is difficult to make predictions, especially about the future. Weather forecaster. Building castles in the air. Can't see the forest for the trees.

48 (Eight of Cups) The meaning of life. Who am I? Why am I here? What is the meaning of life? What's this life for? Your calling in life. Soul searching. Self-discovery. Finding

yourself. Seek and ye shall find. You rock! Rock on. Rockin' out. Dark night of the soul. There's got to be more to life than this. Walking away from it all. It's not about the destination – it's about the journey. If you don't know where you're going any road will take you there. Where are you headed? Long-haul trucking. Tractor-trailer. Forgetting about it all. To want to forget something is to remember it. Just living for today/the day. "Look at the birds of the air; they do not sow or reap or stow away in barns, and yet your heavenly Father feeds them. Are you not much more valuable than they?" God gives every bird a worm, but he does not throw it into the nest. Send out into the world. How to go to heaven, not how the heavens go. What really matters. What's the point? Where is this going? Going nowhere. Headed in the right/wrong direction. I'm outta here. Wasting time. You're throwing your life away.

49 (Nine of Cups) Be satisfied. Life is sweet. Living the life of Riley. It's a piece of cake. Nothing satisfies like satisfaction. Getting what you want. Here's what I want. Grant your wish. Waving a magic wand. Having your cake and eating it too. Icing on the cake. Treat you nice. [Spouse tends to be exceedingly attractive]. Why say no if you can say yes? If I could, I would wave a magic wand and grant your wish. Are you happy now that you've gotten what you wanted? Be careful what you wish for – you just might get it. An eater. Having a sweet tooth. Sugar is sweet. I've got mine. I've had my fill. You can't have your cake and eat it too. What makes you think you could satisfy me? Fat & happy.

50 (Ten of Cups) The joys of family life. Family time. Family ties. We are family. One big family. We are the world. We the people. It's a wonderful life. This is how good life can be. It's a small world. Think global, act local. We are all. We are many. Natural surroundings. Joy to the world. Peace on Earth. Big fish. Plate tectonics. The fuller the cup, the sooner the spill. When it rains it pours. Torrential rain. Broken home.

51 (King of Swords) Live right life. Do the right thing. Taking the high road. Be honest. Be logical. Face facts. A lesson lived is a lesson learned. Practice what you preach. Don't burn your bridges. Code of conduct. Be respectful. Hitting the nail on the head. Calling a spade a spade. Say what you mean, and mean what you say. Words mean things. Solemn word. State your case. Just the facts. On the record. It's official. The ends don't justify the means. The cold, hard facts. Matter of fact. Cut and dry. Obey the law. Upholding the law. Rule of law. Following the letter of the law. By the book. Truth is harsh. Sticks and stones may break my bones, but names will never hurt me. A name doesn't harm us if we don't harm the name. Virtue is its own reward. Give credit where credit is due. There is no price for good advice. Honor is better than honors. New officials introduce strict measures. Honesty is the best policy. Look me in the eye and say that. Men hold the buffalo by its rope and a ruler by his words. New lords, new laws. Neither break a law nor make one. An Act of Congress. Oath of office. Enforcing the rules. Standard operating procedure. Good cop / bad cop. Name and date of birth. Name, rank and serial number. Assign a number. Math whiz. I'm good/bad with numbers. Check your

math. The numbers don't lie. Units of measure. Political office. Elected official. Oath of office. Sworn oath. Sworn official. Commander in chief. When you speak, you never speak twice. There are rules. No one is above the law. No exemptions. No exceptions. The exception proves the rule. A law unto yourself. Red tape. Thou shall not kill. Armed & dangerous. Body count.

52 (Queen of Swords) Tell the truth. If you don't have something nice to say, then don't say anything at all. Some things are better left unsaid. Having to bite your tongue. Nobody's fool. Able to size up people and situations. Backhanded compliments. I'm going to teach you a lesson. Do as I say, not as I do. Saying one thing, but doing another. People in glass houses should not be throwing stones. Look down on. Because I ain't sayin' it don't mean I ain't thinkin' it. Tongue lashing. Name calling. Keep your mouth shut. Shut your mouth. A slap in the face. Hell hath no fury like woman scorned. I told you so. Mirror, mirror on the wall, who's the fairest of them all? Scurrilous rumors. There's no need to talk about yourself – there are plenty of people to do that for you. Gossip needs no carriage. Gossips always suspect that others are talking about them. A patronizing disposition always has its meaner side. Don't insult my intelligence. Lip service. High maintenance. Hyphenated last name. Borderline personality. Bad behavior doesn't justify more bad behavior. Warts and all. Sulfuric acid. Black widow spider.

53 (Knight of Swords) Straight to the point. Cut to the chase/quick. Passionate about your beliefs. Fighting for the truth. Straight to your face with the truth. Being up-front. Having a warrior spirit. With one deft stroke. Convincing argument. Heated discussion. Heated debate. Get on/off your soap box. See things my way. Those convinced against their will are of the same opinion still. Forcing your way of thinking onto others. My way is the only way. One-sided arguments. Fighting over politics. Holier than thou. A war of words. Know-it-all. If your principles don't guide your life, then your life will guide your principles. Usually guilty of doing of what you preach against.

54 (Page of Swords) Ask questions. Monkey see, monkey do. Flying by the seat of your pants. Making it up as you go. Ad lib. Off the cuff. Stand-up comedy. Curiosity killed the cat, but satisfaction brought him back. I am both sides of the coin. Who are you? Identity unknown. Artificial intelligence. Let's watch. Look & see. Check it out. What are you doing? What are you up to? A fly on the wall. I'm all ears. Peek-a-boo, I see you. Tell me what's on your mind. I want to know what you're thinking. Mental telepathy. Remote viewing. Signal to noise. Point of view. A good question is like beating a bell. Fill in the blank. In the form of ______. In the shape of ______. Sounds like ______. Looks like ______. Guessing games. Mental recreation. Mad libs. Wrap your head/mind around this. Cracking the code. Top secret. Change of clothes. Living vicariously. Just go with it. Audio/video. On tape. Roll the tape. Frame by frame. The following has been recorded. This is a recording. Repeat after

me. Remote control. A backup copy. Copy and paste. Logging on. Going online. IT (Information technology). Face to face. Witness/observer. Speaking in the third person. Corroborating witness. Be on the lookout. Looking over your shoulder. Sticking your nose where it doesn't belong. In other words. A play on words. To riff off of something. With a wink and a nod. Talking out of both sides of your mouth. I changed my mind. Wishy-washy. Mirror image. Image reversal. Place side by side. Look-alike. Body double. Often imitated, never duplicated. Role reversal. Back and forth. What she/he said. I couldn't have said it better myself. Putting up a front. Cover story. Things are not as they appear. Living a double life. Assumed identity. Mistaken identity. Baring it all. Messing with your head/mind. Faking it. Fake out. Not knowing what's up and what's down. Laboratory experiments. Petri dish. Massaging the data. Faking it. Cleverness eats its owner. Immature use of the intellect. Mental recreator. Three-dimensional. High resolution. High definition. Blurred vision. Blurring the lines. Pop-out. Exposing yourself. Translators, traitors. Reverse speech. Backward masking. On cue. At the same time. Lip sync. Switch sides. Betrayal of confidence. Slip of the tongue. Can't keep a secret. Loose lips. Tip off. A tell-all. Who knows? Your guess is as good as mine. It's anyone's guess. Mind boggling. Which came first: the chicken or the egg? To spilt into two. Cell membranes. Face off. Face-lift. Case in point. Full disclosure. Information is on a need to know basis. Eyes only. Special ops. Psi ops. A plant. Accentuating the aberrant. Out of the closet. Gender expression. Dude looks like a lady.

55 (Ace of Swords) Think. Use your mind. Open your mind. Free thinking. Open your eyes. Eyes wide open. I can see clearly now. I get it. Truth is self-evident. Knowledge is power. Those who can read see twice as well. A way with words. Food for thought. Feeding your mind. Two heads are better than one. By writing we learn to write. Putting pen to paper. Pad of paper. Pen and ink. Original ideas. New ideas. New solutions. Put your thinking cap on. Problem solving. Mental processing. Mental capacity. Mental strength. That's the idea. That's my idea. Thinking for yourself. Think your own thoughts. In your own words. The contents of the mind. Individual thoughts. Let me be clear. Clearheaded. Clearing your mind. Clear blue skies. There is nothing either good or bad, but thinking makes it so. Constructs of the mind. Good idea. Bad idea. In print. Out of print. It cuts both ways. Might makes right. Be open-minded, but not so open-minded that your brains fall out.

56 (Two of Swords) Blessed are the peacemakers. Be civil. Be diplomatic. I see both sides (of the coin). Not taking sides. I'm just sayin'. I'm just tryin' to say. Striking a delicate balance. Either way it suits me. Remaining neutral. Customer service representative. Social graces. Weighing your options. Make up your mind. Of two minds. Sharing a brain. Head over heart. Cease fire. Peace treaty. Peace at any price. Don't rock the boat. Walking on eggshells. Having to watch your words. Whatever you say, dear. Oh well. Not willing to get your hands dirty. Fence-sitting. I can't decide. Agreeing to disagree. Faux pas.

57 (Three of Swords) I miss you. I'm sad to see you go. I feel your pain. My heart bleeds for you. A heart tried by pain. Harden not your heart. If you know what hurts yourself, you know what hurts others. Wearing your emotions on your sleeve. There's only so many tears you can cry. Quit your whining.

58 (Four of Swords) Be well. Health and wellness. Relax. Give me a break. Leave sleeping dogs lie. Give it a rest. An apple a day keeps the doctor away. Big oaks from little acorns grow. ...and on the seventh day he rested... Take the day off. Day of rest. Take vacation days, not sick days. Regularity is the best medicine. Just what the doctor ordered. No doctor is better than three. Getting a second opinion. Honor physicians before you have need of them. Medical exam. Health checkups. What ails you? Safe haven. Room + bed. Get some therapy. First aid. Medical condition. Medical leave. Sick & tired. I'm sick and tired of being sick and tired. Every invalid is a physician. You made your own bed, now you must lie in it. Out of retirement. Put out to pasture. Civil unrest.

59 (Five of Swords) Picking up the pieces. Salvaging what remains. Cutting your losses. Overcoming self-interest. Aiming for higher consciousness. Clearing negative energy. Treating others the way you would want to be treated. Weathering the storm. Appeasing the gods. The Anointed One. The chosen one. Turning the other cheek. Chain reaction. Personal interests. Personal failings. Accepting defeat. Here's mud in your eye. My God, my God, why have you forsaken me? Everything falls apart. Swallow pride, accept defeat, pick up the pieces – you've been beat. Forcible swallowing of pride. Losing face. Every man for himself. Looking out for number 1. It's all about me. Fall from grace. Finders keepers, losers weepers. Going negative. Scorched earth policy. Winning at any cost. Sore loser. You lose. The agony of defeat. Na, na, na, na. More than you. Better than you. Mumbo jumbo. You cannot damage a wrecked ship. The junk capsizes and the shark has its bellyful. We each have our own crosses to bear. Do unto others what has been done to you. Ream/rip/tear you a new one. The rippin' and the tearin'. Take apart. Piece by piece. A thorn in my side. Falling on your sword.

60 (Six of Swords) Move forward. Leave your troubles behind. Put it behind you. The lay of the land. The road less travelled. Going out of your way. Far off the beaten path. Nook and cranny. Marching to the beat of a different drummer. Thinking outside of the box. Don't fence me in. Trying to pin you down. Putting a check mark in the "Other" box. One of a kind. Push the envelope. Looking forward to it. The long term. Rites of passage. It's a long way away. The journey of 1000 miles begins with a single step. Like a bridge over troubled water. Float downstream. Safe passage. Going abroad. Going places. Third World. Stranger in a strange land. Don't talk to strangers. Approach/avoid. Just go away. Leave me alone. Quit bothering me. Doesn't fit neatly in a box. Not part of the program. Out in left field. Outside of the mainstream. Outside of the parameters. Out of the ordinary. Freak of nature. Like an animal. Trying to stay afloat. Swimming upstream/against the flow. Out of bounds. Out of

line. Going overboard. Opt out. Whose presence does no good, their absence does no harm. Noxious weeds. Land mines. Booby traps. Opposing views. Point/counterpoint. I won't do what you tell me. Border dispute. It's complicated. Sever ties. Going your separate ways. Permanent loss of relationship. This is the last time we'll see each other. Heads are gonna roll. Off with their heads.

61 (Seven of Swords) If you fail to plan, you plan to fail. Doing the unexpected. Having a back up plan (in case plans fall through at the last minute). Having plan B up your sleeve. Staying one step ahead. Exit ramp. Downhill skiing. Cool runnings. Having a trick up your sleeve. I don't fall for that trick. I'm outta here. On the run. Escape unharmed. Sneak by. Slide by. Fit through. Fit in between. Let me sneak by you. Disappearing act. Without a trace. The one that got away. M.I.A. Slip through your fingers. Slip away. Slip and slide. Slip and fall. Fall flat. Slippery slope. Shirking responsibility. Thou shall not steal. Like a thief in the night. The person who steals once is always a thief. Breaking and entering. This is a stick up. Slink away. Head for the hills. On the lam. Leaving tracks. Foiled plans. The best laid plans of mice and men...

62 (Eight of Swords) Facing your fears and overcoming them. Dealing with restrictions. Doing what's unpopular. Boo and hiss. Rattle your cage. Goose bumps. Giving me the chills. Frozen in fear. Like a deer in the headlights. Scared straight. Scare the crap out of you. Snakes bite. Locker room. Under lock and key. The key that opens is also the key that locks. Lock/unlock the door. Open/close the door. Capture and release. Cuff and stuff. Jail cell. Prison cell. Behind bars. I've created my own prison. Lock you up and throw away the key. Locked out. The door is ajar. Hold open. Holding your breath. I can't breathe. Moaning and groaning. Choke hold. Flush the toilet. Roto-rooter. Plugged up. Clogged up. Intergluteal cleft. Shedding skin.

63 (Nine of Swords) No worries. Don't worry. Make the world a better place in which to live. Do your best and let God worry 'bout the rest. "What if?" thinking. Who knows? Misery loves company. Weeping and gnashing of teeth. Worried sick. It's a pity. Talking about dire matters. Mental torture. Last resort. Intensive care unit. Under the knife.

64 (Ten of Swords) Undoing ruin. All is not lost. The darkness before the dawn. The worst is over. A karmic drama that just needs to be played out to its conclusion. Misfortune is not that which can be avoided, but that which cannot. Ice cubes. On the rocks. Block of ice. White noise. Dragging you down. Bummed out. This sucks. It's the pits. Hitting rock bottom. Darkest hour. Will there ever be an end? To the end. The end complete. Final curtain. It's done. It's all over. Stick a fork in it. There's nothing you can do about it. Going behind your back. Snow and ice. Gloom and doom. We're closed.

65 (King of Pentacles) Calculate. Do the math. Making it big time. Making your mark. Show me the money. Brains and brawn. Everything you touch turns to gold. Having the Midas touch. Top of the world. King of kings. Big shot. Calling the shots. Big business. Making bank. Large sums of money. Mother lode. Better a diamond with a flaw than a pebble without one. Diamonds are priceless. All that glitters is not gold. Rare earth minerals. Precious metals, stones, gems, and jewels. No nickname, no wealth. Money talks. Deep pockets. Upping the ante. Ante up. High stakes. I'm all in. A bet is a bet. Shooting/playing pool. Pit bulls. When gold talks, speech is useless. That is gold which is worth gold. A diamond on a dunghill is a precious diamond still. Piggy bank. Living large. Flaunting your wealth. Flash the cash. Paying through the nose. Pick you up and shake you upside down. Getting a piece of the pie. There is safety in numbers. Keep it in the family. The fix is in. In your back pocket. Pocketing the cash. Buy off. Follow the money. Calling your bluff. Totally blowing it. Working blue. Body odor. Ganging up on. Flash mob.

66 (Queen of Pentacles) Managing your money. Making good investments. Bringing home the bacon. Cash cow. Golden goose. Overcoming fear of failure. Overcoming suspicion of others.

67 (Knight of Pentacles) Slow and steady wins the race. Daily routines. Doing the laundry. Mowing the lawn. Raking the leaves. Shoveling snow. Another day, another dollar. Working 9 to 5. The daily grind. Toiling away. Paying the bills. Home economics. Personal economics. The unwashed, unlettered masses. Labour warms, sloth harms. Your average slob.

68 (Page of Pentacles) Study. Learn. Do your homework. Get an education. The value of learning. Worth learning. Worth studying. Scholars are the treasure of a nation. Money for school. High priced education. Grade point average. Education don't come by bumping against the schoolhouse.

69 (Ace of Pentacles) Make money. To have is to have, but the art is to get. You get what you pay for. Price you pay. What's it worth to you? Making it worth your while. Expensive tastes. Suit & tie. Hair is parted to the side. Whatever works. Whatever it takes. Go with what you know. Valuable resources. What costs nothing is worth nothing.

70 (Two of Pentacles) Be flexible. Handling change. On a shoestring budget.

71 (Three of Pentacles) Doing a good job. Quality is job 1. A job well done. Good at what you do. Without tools no handicraft. A bad workman quarrels with his tools. A bad workman blames his tools.

72 (Four of Pentacles) A penny saved is a penny earned. Every penny counts. Save it – you may need it. Savings account. Take care of the nickels and dimes, and the dollars take care of themselves. If you want to double your money, fold it in half and put it back in your pocket. The millionaire mind. Accumulated wealth. Get rich slow. Living on less than you earn. The tried & true. Maintaining the status quo. Same old, same old. Business as usual. No need to impress you. Living on the cheap. Like a dragon sitting on a pile of gold.

73 (Five of Pentacles) Gainfully employed. You're hired. Waste not, want not. Having a roof over your head. Fix-it shops. Cobble together. Economic hardship. Material troubles. Enduring hardship. Doing without. Going without. Toughing it out. Making due. Tough times. Hard times. Economic downturn. Out in the cold. Exposure to the elements. Spare change? Low income. You're fired. Laid off. Unemployment compensation. Workplace injury. Broken bones. It's not so bad to fall in the gutter, but it's worse to lay there. Hard luck story. Stinking bum. Trash can. Take out the trash. Garbage in, garbage out. Throw away. Kick it to the curb. Dumpster diving. Throw the bums out. Hungry bellies have no ears. There are none so deaf as those who will not hear. I'm starvin'. Burning down the house.

74 (Six of Pentacles) Share wisely. Giving to those who deserve. We want more. Heart of gold. Gift giving. Give with discretion, accept with memory. The gifts you have been given. The gift carries the giver. The gift that keeps on giving. Gifts with strings attached. It is better to give than to receive. Give it away. Economic disparity. Sense of entitlement. Objects of charity. Penny wise, pound foolish. Spreading the wealth. Folks is mighty generous with money they ain't got. Purse-proud. Less than charitable.

75 (Seven of Pentacles) Calm down. Be patient. Patience is a virtue. You reap what you sow. Looking for the day when you receive the fruits of your labor. Don't anticipate. Rome was not built in a day. More trouble than it's worth. Heavy losses. Conspiracy theories. No one is out to get me. Out to get you.

76 (Eight of Pentacles) Be efficient. Going directly from point A to point B. The shortest distance between two points is a straight line. Get the job done. Getting things done. Get 'r done. Crank it out. Knockin' 'em down. Getting things lined up. Getting all your ducks in a row. Running a tight ship.

77 (Nine of Pentacles) Pray on the matter. Now what? What do I do next? Hands pressed together. Alone with your wealth.

78 (Ten of Pentacles) Be wealthy. Build vast family wealth. Accumulation of wealth. Changing your financial family tree.

Please feel free to contact the author:

petersoned@hotmail.com

A depiction of the contents of this book is at:

http://numerologybasics.com/

Special thanks to Mike Byrne, Tony Cohen, Jesse Noe, Adam Clark, Amy Herring, Verena Heinrich, William Brabam and Stacy Lawson.

14204227R00024

Printed in Poland
by Amazon Fulfillment
Poland Sp. z o.o., Wrocław